IMAGES OF WAR

THE FRENCH ARMY
IN THE
FIRST WORLD WAR

Saint-Thomas-en-Argonne (Marne), 25 July 1915. Resting on a copy of *Le Petit Parisien*, a popular national daily, a Provençal soldier from 255th Infantry writes a letter.

IMAGES OF WAR

THE FRENCH ARMY IN THE FIRST WORLD WAR

RARE PHOTOGRAPHS FROM WARTIME ARCHIVES

Ian Sumner

Pen & Sword
MILITARY

First published in Great Britain in 2016 by
PEN & SWORD MILITARY
an imprint of
Pen & Sword Books Ltd,
47 Church Street,
Barnsley,
South Yorkshire
S70 2AS

Text copyright © Pen & Sword, 2016

Every effort has been made to trace the copyright of all the photographs. If there are unintentional omissions, please contact the publisher in writing, who will correct all subsequent editions.

A CIP record for this book is available from the British Library.

ISBN 978 147385 619 6

The right of Ian Sumner to be identified as Author of this Work has been asserted by him in accordance with the Copyright, Designs and Patents Act 1988.

All rights reserved. No part of this book may be reproduced or transmitted in any form or by any means, electronic or mechanical including photocopying, recording or by any information storage and retrieval system, without permission from the Publisher in writing.

Typeset by CHIC GRAPHICS

Printed and bound by CPI Group (UK) Ltd, Croydon, CR0 4YY

Pen & Sword Books Ltd incorporates the imprints of Pen & Sword Archaeology, Atlas, Aviation, Battleground, Discovery, Family History, History, Maritime, Military, Naval, Politics, Railways, Select, Social History, Transport, True Crime, Claymore Press, Frontline Books, Leo Cooper, Praetorian Press, Remember When, Seaforth Publishing and Wharncliffe.

For a complete list of Pen & Sword titles please contact
Pen & Sword Books Limited
47 Church Street, Barnsley, South Yorkshire, S70 2AS, England
E-mail: enquiries@pen-and-sword.co.uk
Website: www.pen-and-sword.co.uk

Contents

Introduction and Acknowledgements 7

Chapter One
    'The attack must be pursued at close quarters' 9

Chapter Two
    Finding the Right Formula 28

Chapter Three
    'Warriors ready for anything' 60

Chapter Four
    'We know nothing of glory' 76

Chapter Five
    'Life goes on' 102

Chapter Six
    'An unforgettable day' 122

Contents

Introduction and Acknowledgements 7

Chapter One
'The attack must be pursued at close quarters' 9

Chapter Two
Finding the Right Formula 28

Chapter Three
'Warriors ready for anything' 60

Chapter Four
'We know nothing of glory' 76

Chapter Five
'Life goes on' 102

Chapter Six
'An unforgettable day' 122

Introduction and Acknowledgements

The First World War demanded an enormous effort of France and its people. During the course of the fighting, eight-and-a-half million Frenchmen were mobilized – 40 per cent of all males and 60 per cent of those of working age – to serve alongside 260,000 North Africans and 215,000 colonials. One-and-a-half million men were killed – on average 890 a day – and three million wounded, including 800,000 left disabled for life. At the same time French industry and agriculture was damaged by invasion and subsequent manpower shortages. Yet still the nation rallied. Food supplies were maintained, industry was transformed into a machine capable of supporting a vast ongoing military endeavour, and a fierce determination to drive the invader from French soil eventually produced a bitter victory. France shouldered the heaviest burden of all the Allies, and the legacy of the conflict continued to affect its politics and society for years to come.

This book is not an illustrated chronology of the conflict. Instead, it concentrates on the experience of the French soldier, in the trenches and behind the lines, forming a graphic companion to my earlier work *They Shall Not Pass: the French Army on the Western Front, 1914–1918* (Pen & Sword, 2012). We follow the soldier into the front line and out again. Chapter 1 covers mobilization and the battles of 1914, as well as call-up, training and departure for the front – an experience shared by millions over the next four years. Chapter 2 explores front-line combat, including technological innovation and the treatment of casualties; Chapter 3, the mundane realities of trench life. Chapter 4 considers front-line attitudes to the enemy, to France's allies and to other corps – as well as the vital role played by the artillery, engineers, transport and the rest in the final victory. Chapter 5 concentrates on time out of the front line, including rest, leave and medical treatment in the rear. Chapter 6 ends with a view of the armistice and demobilization – a time of celebration, of readjustment to civilian life and, for many, an uncertain future.

Wherever possible, these eloquent images are supported by extracts translated by the author from contemporary diaries, letters and newspapers – the immediate, first-hand testimony, uncoloured by hindsight or lapses of memory, previously highlighted in *They Shall Not Pass*.

I would like to thank all who have helped in the writing of *The French Army in the First World War*, particularly my wife Margaret, for her translating and editing skills, but also the staffs of the Service Historique de la Défense at Vincennes, the Bibliothèque Nationale in Paris, the municipal libraries of Albi, Dijon, Meaux and Tours, and the British Library. As in my previous title in the 'Images of War' series, *The French Army at Verdun* (Pen & Sword, 2016), the photographs used are drawn from the exceptionally rich archive of French official photographs at the Bibliothèque de Documentation Internationale et Contemporaine, Université de Paris-Nanterre. My gratitude goes to them and to the following named photographers:

Captain André: 35 (top)
Lieutenant Barbier: 82 (bottom)
Lieutenant Bied: 69 (top)
Branger: 14 (top), 31 (top)
Lieutenant Candlot: 31 (bottom), 90 (bottom)
Chambrin: 65
Lieutenant Champagne: 87, 95 (top)
G. Cherau: 12 (top)
Clair-Guyot: 12 (bottom)
Lieutenant Desaulle: 34 (top)
Durand: 55 (bottom)
Dr Gallier: 49 (top)
Golweiss-Leroy: 14 (bottom)
Lieutenant Guillardot: 32 (top), 38 (top), 43

Captain J. Heilbronner: 64 (top)
Houtart: 16 (top)
Captain Lagarde: 46 (bottom), 47
Captain Le Mintier: 84 (bottom)
Léré: 67 (bottom), 88 (bottom)
Manuel: 13 (bottom)
Sergeant Mathieu: 15 (bottom)
M. Plagnes: 59 (top)
Lieutenant de Preissac: 46 (top), 67 (top), 94 (bottom), 124 (top)
Reims: 16 (bottom)
Rey: 81 (bottom)
Lieutenant Colonel Seauve: 85 (bottom)
Dr Simon: 104 (top)
Tournyol du Clos: 48

Every effort has been made to avoid infringing copyright and all exceptions are unintentional. If this has occurred, please notify the publisher, who will include the appropriate credit in future editions or reprints.

Chapter One

'The attack must be pursued at close quarters'

In contrast to its British counterpart, the French army that mobilized in August 1914 was manned by conscription. Every 20-year-old male was liable for three years' service with the colours, followed by eleven as a reservist and fourteen as a territorial – each annual class of conscripts comprising between 250,000 and 300,000 men. The opening battles were fought by the three annual 'classes' of 1911, 1912 and 1913, yielding a force of some 90,000 officers and 817,000 men. They would soon be followed by the class of 1914, summoned two months in advance of its October call-up, and then by the classes of 1915 to 1919, all conscripted early, some by as much as twenty-one months. Conscript, soldier or reservist, every man received a big send-off when his regiment or draft left the barracks, usually for the local railway station. While the bands played famous old tunes like the *Sambre et Meuse* or the *Chant du départ*, cheering crowds gathered, offering the soldiers flowers and kisses. Civilians and soldiers alike sometimes struck up the *Marseillaise* or the popular *Quand Madelon*. The chasseurs, however, had their own song – *Sidi Brahim*.

In line with prevailing French military orthodoxy, the commander-in-chief, General Joseph Joffre, was determined to attack – and to attack using his infantry. The strategy was vaunted to be in the 'best traditions' of the army and to suit the 'French psyche', victory resulting not from superior tactics nor yet superior weaponry, but from superior will. Both cavalry and artillery had been relegated to ancillary roles – the artillery to provide fire support for the ground troops; the cavalry to reconnoitre the field before withdrawing in anticipation of the decisive intervention and pursuit – and in consequence French weapons development had concentrated on field artillery, in the shape of the 75mm gun, rather than the howitzers and heavy guns favoured by the Germans. An infantry battalion would move into contact by throwing out a preliminary line of skirmishers, holding the remainder of its troops in columns in reserve. Once contact was made, the reserves would be fed into the firing line, first to suppress the hostile guns; then, helped by the field artillery, to inflict enough casualties to force the enemy line to waver. Finally, a bayonet charge would deliver the coup de grace. 'To be decisive and irresistible, the attack must be pursued at close quarters,' claimed the 1913 infantry regulations. 'The supreme weapon of the infantryman is the bayonet.'

The regulations also struck a note of caution: 'the infantry', they warned, 'must be employed with prudence'. Many French officers, however, overlooked such caveats. Shortage of both funds and big training grounds had limited pre-war opportunities for large-scale field exercises – to the evident frustration of General Lyautey, then French commander in Morocco. 'There is little point in revising the regulations or advocating the offensive in all its forms,' he complained, 'unless and until we address our chronic lack of provision for field training.' Training took place largely at regimental level, while the four-year round of manoeuvres for larger formations – brigade level in years one and two, army corps level in year three, and army level in year four – ensured that no conscript would ever serve through a complete cycle. Reservists were recalled for training twice a year, for periods of twenty-three days and seventeen days respectively; the territorials, for one nine-day period; the territorial reserves, for just one day.

The consequences quickly made themselves apparent. In late August 1914, during the string of indecisive meeting engagements collectively entitled the battles of the Frontiers, the French infantry sallied forth without adequate reconnaissance or artillery support; and with each fifty or so strong platoon distributed in pairs across a front of 100 to 200 metres, the skirmish line proved too widely spaced for effective command. 'Every unit coming into contact with the enemy resolved at once to charge forward, taking the initiative if no order was received,' commented a post-war account of the battle of Charleroi (22 August). 'The decision was almost automatic, the product of reflex not reason.' In practice it was guns, not bayonets, that proved conclusive. The French had grossly underestimated German firepower; and lacking howitzers and heavy artillery, they had nothing to counter the enemy guns, which were able to fire with impunity behind any kind of crest.

Joffre reacted immediately, sacking 162 generals at all levels of command – so clearing the way for the likes of Ferdinand Foch, Émile Fayolle and Philippe Pétain – and within a fortnight the Germans had been halted at the battle of the Marne: 'If my action was crowned with success,' remarked the commander-in-chief, 'it is largely because by early September our armies had progressed since the start of the war. Despite the loss of so many officers and NCOs, the infantry had learned from the bitter experience of the battles of the Frontiers. They made better use of the terrain, understood the value of the tools at their disposal and showed a greater willingness to use them, and no longer went into action without artillery support.' Yet still the decisive blow remained elusive. In a series of attempted outflanking manoeuvres, each side tried to leapfrog the other heading towards the coast, but this 'Race to the Sea' ended in stalemate. By late September men were digging shelter trenches, and by November a network of parallel trenches ran from the Channel to the Swiss border.

The number of casualties incurred in these early battles was appalling. By the end of 1914, 301,000 French soldiers had been killed, 240,000 in August and September alone. Some regiments had lost almost half their fighting strength of 2,700: by November 1914, for example, 74th Infantry included 1,175 replacements; 129th Infantry, 1,345. To replace the losses, the class of 1914 was thrown quickly – probably too quickly – into the field: 'Combat training is very rudimentary,' noted a report on 74th Infantry in late 1914. 'At the depot, knowledge of the present conflict is scant. The men say they only fire their rifles once a week. The volunteers from Alsace can't shoot.' Passing through a village in early 1915, Lieutenant Maurice Genevoix (106th Infantry) spotted a column of troops. A working party of territorials, he thought initially. But no, it was a new draft from the class of 1914: 'Their greatcoats were too big for them and slipping from their shoulders. They carried their pack too high, chafing the nape of the neck. Staring straight ahead, they rubbed the sore patch – some pale, eyes blank, others red-faced, sweating profusely despite the cold.' One of Genevoix's friends was standing nearby. 'They're willing and that will take them so far,' he remarked. 'It's not enough, though. [Their enthusiasm] will soon evaporate . . . [They're] young, far too young.'

Training did develop progressively over the course of the conflict. French headquarters staff quickly distilled and distributed the tactical lessons of the early combats, meanwhile hoping that accumulated trench *savoir faire* would be conveyed by veterans to newcomers – a plan thwarted in the short term by the continued high level of casualties. During the summer of 1915 a number of infantry schools were created within each army to improve and standardize training procedures. Then in 1916 one battalion per division was designated as a training unit, operating in specialist and general schools based in purpose-built camps – a structure further developed by General Pétain, commander-in-chief from May 1917, to include courses in inter-arms cooperation and senior command.

Versailles (Yvelines), 3 August 1914. The mobilization decree was issued on 1 August, to take effect the following day. Here, a 75mm gun belonging to 22nd Artillery (6th Infantry Division) passes the famous palace en route to its mobilization station. The gun has just left the regimental barracks on the Avenue de Sceaux and would soon be firing in earnest. By late August the division was in action at Charleroi and Guise, then in September on the Marne.

Paris, 3 August 1914. Dragoons trot through a crowded Place de l'Opéra. A number of dragoon regiments were garrisoned in and around the city: 5th (Compiègne), 7th (Fontainebleau), 23rd (Vincennes) and 27th (Versailles).

Bar-le-Duc (Meuse), 6 September 1914. Troops leave for the front from the station. The town was home to 94th Infantry (VI Corps, 42nd Division) and 294th Infantry (56th Reserve Division), as well as a detachment of 154th Infantry. The men of 94th Infantry were soon in action – in August around Charleroi and in September on the Marne. So too were the reservists of 294th Infantry, first on the Marne and then the Aisne.

Paris, 1914. An Algerian tirailleur regiment marches to the front. On the outbreak of war the French immediately formed four divisions from troops already serving in north Africa (37th, 38th, 45th and Moroccan.) Transported to France during the second week of August, they were soon in action in Lorraine and on the Marne.

Paris, 1914. A unit of naval infantry marches through the city. Sailors, mainly Breton reservists, had been the first troops assigned to defend the capital, their uniform and equipment betraying their hurried departure: 'We didn't have any greatcoats and left Brest in our jumpers. We even had to jury rig our own equipment braces out of cord. The captain had no holster for his revolver and carried it on a lanyard. And the rifles from the stores in the Brest arsenal looked all right, but in practice half the springs were broken.' Formed into an infantry brigade, that first draft was all but wiped out in fierce fighting in the autumn of 1914, defending the line of the Yser around the Flemish town of Diksmuide.

Creil (Oise), 2 September 1914. The French destroyed several bridges to slow the enemy advance, including this key crossing of the Oise, guarding the northern approaches to Paris. Here, 1st Engineers had acted just in time; fifteen minutes later the German advance guard reached the river. The Germans briefly occupied Creil, an important railway junction, but evacuated the town after the battle of the Marne. A temporary bridge put up by the French Engineers was eventually replaced in 1922; this new structure was twice destroyed in the Second World War – in 1940 and 1944 – and permanently rebuilt in 1948.

Near Anglure (Marne), September 1914. A column marches north, en route to the Marne battlefield. As a bridging point of the Aube, the town was a potential gateway to the Seine valley and Paris, and thus the objective of a German Guards Corps division. However, the tenacious French defence on the Marne kept it safe from enemy attack.

Berry-au-Bac (Aisne), 16 September 1914. A column of 6th Infantry heads towards the firing line during the battle of the Aisne. Walking wounded from 236th Infantry (left) plod back to the railhead at Jonchery-sur-Vesle (Marne), while a group of medical orderlies (right) observe proceedings. Behind is the Chemin des Dames ridge and the village of Craonne, the scene of the catastrophic French offensive of April 1917.

Cons-la-Grandville (Meurthe-et-Moselle), 24 August 1914. Tirailleurs of the Moroccan Division enjoy welcome refreshment en route to the front. The Moroccan Division arrived in France on 18 August; by 23 August it had reached Mézières (Ardennes), and just five days later went into action at nearby Dommery. By a tradition developed in north Africa and other French overseas territories, a soldier on campaign carried as much as he could about his person. Hanging from the straps of his personal equipment were three cartridge pouches, a leather pack and a bayonet frog, while crossed over his chest were a haversack and water bottle. Each man also had an extra burden to bear: a cooking pot (each section carried six) or one of the company tools (pickaxe, spade, shears or axe) and possibly a tent section. According to its precise composition, the load weighed anything between 25 and 28kg.

Carency (Pas-de-Calais), 27 December 1914. Chasseurs alpins from General Pétain's XXXIII Corps move forward in the second wave of this attack; the first wave is just visible on the horizon (right). Advancing behind a heavy bombardment, six battalions of chasseurs and one of line infantry took the enemy first line, but German counter-attacks the following day forced them back almost to their start line. Further follow-up action was stymied by bad weather.

General Joseph Joffre (1852–1931), Chantilly (Oise), January 1916. For most front-line soldiers, generals were remote figures; only Joffre and Pétain were at all well known. Here, General Joffre, the French commander-in-chief, leaves his HQ alongside General Sir Douglas Haig, the recently appointed commander of the British Expeditionary Force. The two men were thrashing out the details of a joint Somme offensive for the coming summer; its failure would later cost Joffre his job.

General Joseph Gallieni (1849–1916), Paris, April 1915. Gallieni, an experienced colonial soldier recalled to duty at the outbreak of war, is pictured here outside the Trocadéro. As military governor of Paris, he was responsible for defending the capital, and troops under his command played a decisive role during the battle of the Marne in September 1914. In October 1915 Gallieni became minister of war, but the strain of high office broke his already fragile health and he died only seven months later.

Paris, September 1915. Beset by paper, the men of 22nd Administration Company are hard at work in the mobilization office at La Tour Maubourg barracks, situated immediately behind the Hôtel des Invalides. The documents stacked on the desks and shelves are all personnel files.

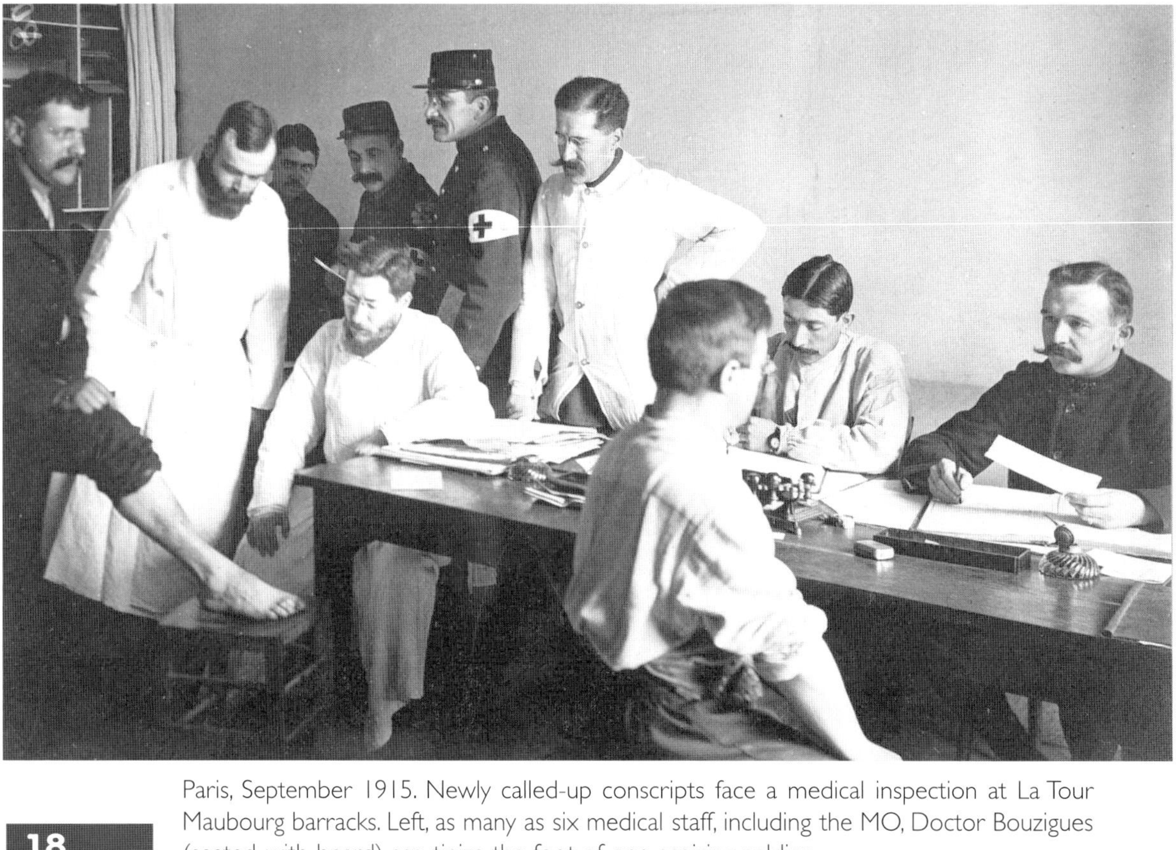

Paris, September 1915. Newly called-up conscripts face a medical inspection at La Tour Maubourg barracks. Left, as many as six medical staff, including the MO, Doctor Bouzigues (seated, with beard) scrutinize the foot of one aspiring soldier.

Paris, 11 January 1916. Young men of the class of 1917 leave from the Gare d'Austerlitz, bound for regimental depots in the south-west. Their call-up notices had been sent out four days earlier, a full twenty-one months before the prescribed date of October 1917. Slogans are chalked on the side of the carriage in French ('Vive la classe') and English ('Class of the Victory').

Paris, 11 January 1916. At another main railway terminal, the Gare de Montparnasse, parents pack the forecourt and balcony to take leave of their sons. 'We are Frenchmen and anxious to do our duty, so this is no time to flinch in front of our comrades,' wrote Henri Despeyrières (14th Infantry). 'No sadness is allowed. In public we try to act tough.'

Paris, 18 April 1918. Conscripts from the class of 1919 gather outside the Gare de Montparnasse, bound for regimental depots in Normandy and Brittany. Placards indicate their respective destinations: Alençon (Orne), Rennes (Ille-et-Vilaine) and Saint-Brieuc (Côtes d'Armor). In August 1914 the parish priest of Martigné-Ferchaud (Ille-et-Vilaine) had watched the men of this tiny Breton village leave for their regiment (probably 70th Infantry in Vitré): 'Tears were undoubtedly shed as [they] said their last goodbyes . . . shortly afterwards, as they moved away, they burst into patriotic songs, which echoed briefly, then all that could be heard was the noise of the engine.'

Paris, 9 January 1916. Caps flying, bottles in hand, conscripts from the class of 1917 prepare to leave a goods station, the Gare d'Ivry-Marchandises, for regimental depots in the south-west. 'There are around thirty, an assortment of caps, hats and berets. There's even a topper and a priest's hat, the latter belonging to a seminarian who, taking his bishop's advice, has insisted on turning up in clerical garb. Each man carries a bag or knotted handkerchief containing a change of clothes. Most popular of all, probably because some reservist recommended it, is the small, yellow, mock-canvas, cardboard suitcase that has become the French soldier's luggage of choice – on leave, on discharge or on recall from the reserve. The top hat, however, is carrying a magnificent travelling bag with nickel-plated clasps.'

Depot of 1st Zouaves, Reuil (Marne), January 1916. The four zouave regiments were originally raised for service in north Africa, but all opened a depot on home soil after August 1914. Here, a barracks-room stands ready to accommodate conscripts from the class of 1917. 'Chivvied as ever by the corporal, their real mentor, the recruits find their allotted spot, then set off down the corridors, quickly returning burdened under mattress, bolster, coverlet and a pair of sheets. It looks like a line of market porters is invading the room. The next task is to construct the bed – a frame of two iron trestles, to which is fixed, after much fiddling, the mesh fancifully described as the springs. The veterans feel duty bound to offer the benefit of their experience, but always under the beady eye of the corporal, who carries the can for any damage to the fixtures and fittings.'

Reuil (Marne), January 1916. The showers at the depot of 1st Zouaves present an equally spartan picture. 'Once a week men proceed to the infirmary to take a warm shower, six or eight at a time under a circle of heads that spray them with a reviving – but normally unwelcome – rain. The corporal favours a methodical approach to showering his section ... commanding this unarmed drill as if he was on the parade ground – right turn, left turn, about face – basting the men like spit-roasted chickens.'

Camp de l'Étoile, Saint-Crépin-aux-Bois (Oise), February 1918. New recruits of the class of 1919 are put through their paces. For the first two months the training programme aimed to instil a basic level of fitness and concentrated on developing individual skills. It then increased in intensity to equip a man for life on campaign. Here, men perform knee-bends while carrying two 10kg sandbags across the shoulders; other exercises involved running and crawling while similarly laden. 'I shouldn't have made fun of gymnastics; nor should we have laughed at the gym clubs you used to see on a Sunday. It's amazing how moving like a drunken frog contrives to loosen you up. I was blowing like a pair of bellows to start with. Now I'm a butterfly. As for all the peasants who lumber around as if they've 100 kilos of lead in the seat of their trousers, the transformation is remarkable. [Gymnastics] really does liven men up. The carthorses are all skipping around like rabbits.'

Camp de l'Étoile, Saint-Crépin-aux-Bois (Oise), February 1918. New recruits practice boxing. The drill shown here was designed to 'develop strength, agility, alertness and composure, train the nervous system, boost the respiratory and circulatory systems and develop endurance and resistance to pain'. French boxing does not adhere to the Queensbury Rules and allows kicking. 'The best part is learning how to punch and kick so as to break all your opponent's limbs one by one. I recommend the roundhouse kick, old chap. Beware the hind legs!'

Camp de Chéry-Chartreuve (Aisne), July 1917. Senegalese troops receive instruction in bayonet fencing: '"At ease," commands [Corporal] Bougonneau. He adopts the "en garde" position, knees bent, and repeats the different movements, announcing each in turn and combining them with great agility. He performs a "right turn" while pointing, then an "en tête, parry" after taking two steps back, expertly mimicking combat first against an infantryman and then a cavalryman. His ripostes are crisp, his thrusts decisive. He would make a formidable opponent in hand-to-hand combat. Then comes time for individual practice, the pupils rehearsing the movements demonstrated by the master.'

Camp de l'Étoile, Saint-Crépin-aux-Bois (Oise), February 1918. Conscripts from the class of 1919 practise musketry work. For much of the conflict, the basic infantry weapon remained the obsolescent 8mm Lebel rifle, originally designed in 1886 and modified in 1896. Although robust and accurate, it was no match for the enemy Mausers and Mannlichers, mainly due to its magazine. Loading the gun was a laborious process, with eight separate rounds pushed singly down a tube bored in the fore-end. Reloading was necessarily slow, and the gun's centre of gravity changed with every shot, demanding very careful aim. From 1917 the Lebel was progressively replaced by the 1907 Berthier, a version of the standard cavalry carbine, which used three- or five-round clips. So ubiquitous was the Lebel, however, that the full introduction of the Berthier took many months.

Camp de l'Étoile, Saint-Crépin-aux-Bois (Oise), February 1918. Conscripts from the class of 1919 check their targets. Number 1 seems to be firing high and to the left. Although the quality of instruction was deemed good, some recruits remained irredeemably bad shots – a failing attributed to 'inadequate training of the nervous system'. In other words, the shooter flinched at the rifle's report and its recoil into his shoulder. A remedy was suggested, however. The instructor was advised first to accustom the recruit to firing blanks, then sneak in a live round.

Machine-gun school, Fère-en-Tardenois (Aisne). These men are training on a 1914 Hotchkiss, mounted on a Saint-Étienne tripod. The 1897-pattern Hotchkiss had been the first machine gun introduced into the French army. For reasons of economy, it used the same 8mm rounds as the Lebel, held in short aluminium 24-round trays rather than the usual fabric belts. Other types of machine gun followed, but neither the 1905 Puteaux nor the 1907 Saint-Étienne could match the Hotchkiss. Indeed, the Puteaux was markedly less effective, and attempts at improvement succeeded only in making a poor design worse. Exposed to the mud of the Western Front, the Puteaux quickly revealed its shortcomings. It was banished to the colonies, and from 1916 the army returned to the faithful Hotchkiss.

Bombing school, near Cormicy (Marne), August 1916. French bombing courses trained men to lob the grenade, rather than throw it flat, and laid great emphasis on accuracy. The nature of front-line combat had brought the hand grenade into its own, but it was 1916 before the first efficient model, a Billant, was released. Like the British Mills bomb, the Billant was fired by pulling a wire pin to release a lever which rose and ignited the fuse. However, poor quality control and carrying practices – the grenades were normally stowed loose in the infantryman's haversack – meant the levers and pins easily became entangled, and premature explosions were rife.

Machine-gun school, Sapicourt (Marne), September 1916. Trainees learn how to fire the Chauchat light machine gun. Named after its inventor, the gun was originally produced as part of a pre-war programme to develop an automatic rifle. Chauchat had conceived his weapon as something comparable to an artillery piece, favouring the ability to lay down a barrage of fire more highly than shot-by-shot accuracy. The gun was thus designed to be operated at the walk, the firer alongside his number two. To maintain the maximum volume of fire, the magazine had openings in the side to allow easy monitoring of the state of the ammunition. Fine on a test range perhaps, but in the field they simply allowed mud to penetrate the mechanism.

Le Châtelet barracks, Toul (Meurthe-et-Moselle), November 1915. Training complete, men from 55th Chasseurs (121st Division) say farewell to their comrades before leaving for the Aisne, west of Soissons, then a relatively quiet sector of the front line. As a reserve battalion, the 55th was composed of older men. Maurice Maréchal (74th Infantry) and his pals marched away on 2 August 1914: 'I embraced my comrades and the sergeant just before we left. Who knows how many will return? ... No matter: forward!'

Paris, 13 April 1915. Marching along the Rue Royale, a woman accompanies her husband, part of a draft of 23rd Colonial Infantry heading for the Champagne front at the Main de Massiges. Originally raised in France for service in the colonies, the majority of colonial regiments drew their men from the main naval bases on the Atlantic and Mediterranean coasts. However, the 23rd (and the 21st) recruited in Paris. The regiment had already suffered heavy casualties during the battles of the Frontiers in August 1914 and would do so again at Massiges.

Chapter Two

Finding the Right Formula

During the winter of 1914/15 Joffre came under intense political pressure, both to drive the invader from French soil and to relieve Russia on the Eastern Front. Attacks launched between November and January in the Argonne, Artois and Champagne were by later standards relatively small affairs, most involving a single corps, as senior commanders vied for the honour of making the decisive breakthrough. All ended in bloody failure. Joffre next assembled three army corps, supported by 350 guns, to smash their way through the German lines in Artois. In April 1915 they advanced 3km over a 6km front but stalled before a resolute defence. Five months later an even larger force was assembled to attack simultaneously in Artois and Champagne, but these twin offensives also came to naught, stymied yet again by the shortage of heavy artillery.

Small unit tactics remained unchanged. Attacks still comprised a preliminary bombardment designed to disorientate the enemy, followed by a line of infantrymen running towards the trenches to occupy the 'conquered' ground. Instead of 'fire and move' – alternate groups advancing and providing mutual cover with rifle fire – the line went forward as one, as close behind the barrage as possible. With each failed offensive, the preliminary bombardment grew more intense, but to little real effect. Not only did the 75mm field gun lack the range to support the infantry deep within enemy lines, it was also powerless to destroy the enemy wire.

The failures of 1915, with their death toll of almost 350,000 men, the highest annual total of the war, forced a rethink. For 1916, senior commanders like Foch, Fayolle and Pétain began to develop a more methodical, 'scientific' approach, envisaging an offensive as a series of hammer-blows, designed to reduce the enemy positions one by one. On the Somme in July these fresh tactics brought some initial gains, certainly greater than any achieved by the British. However, the new strategy soon proved overly centralized, the pace and form of attacks too often determined by a rigid timetable that gave local commanders no licence to exploit success and the German defenders time to recover. Preparations on the Somme had also been disrupted by events at Verdun, where the sheer weight of the German attack in February 1916 had inevitably pulled in precious French reserves. General Pétain had managed to hold the line, and by October the French were ready to counter-attack, now under the command of former artilleryman General Robert Nivelle.

Nivelle abandoned the tactics of the Somme, introducing instead a series of short, sharp offensives, heavily supported by the artillery over the whole depth of the German positions, and quickly regained much of the ground lost that spring. The French had hung on in 1916, with fewer lives lost (the annual death toll fell by almost 100,0000), but still the breakthrough remained elusive. In December 1916 Joffre was sacked, to be replaced as commander-in-chief by the ebullient Nivelle, who claimed his tactics at Verdun provided 'the right formula' to repeat his success on a wider front. In April 1917 he launched a major offensive on the Aisne, attacking strong German positions on the Chemin des Dames ridge. The result was a disaster, ill-chosen terrain, atrocious weather, lack of resources and poor operational security combining to produce heavy casualties for precious little gain.

Morale was already low after the heroic sacrifices of Verdun and the Somme, and the subsequent failure on the Aisne provoked a paroxysm of indiscipline – protests not against war in general, nor even this war in particular, but against its conduct. Soldiers believed that they were lambs to the slaughter, sacrificed on the altar of futile offensives. Problems of command undoubtedly also played a part, losses among officers and NCOs leading to a shortage of men of experience and good judgement at every level.

In May 1917 Nivelle was sacked in his turn and succeeded by General Pétain. The new commander-in-chief took a novel approach, proposing a series of limited offensives right along the front, supporting his infantry with overwhelming concentrations of artillery, tanks and aircraft, and launching ground attacks only once these were in place. Drawing on his experience at Verdun, where men frequently lost touch with their command posts, he also emphasized marksmanship and self-reliance – concepts previously absent from French infantry training. In Flanders in July, then at La Malmaison (Aisne) in August, his tactics did much to restore morale, minimizing French losses while inflicting significant casualties on the enemy. A total of 164,000 French soldiers were killed in 1917, the lowest annual toll of the war.

Pétain refined his tactics again for 1918, with smaller but better-targeted bombardments and greater use of air power. His aim was to create a series of pockets – 10km deep by 15km wide – within the German lines, so isolating the defenders and forcing them either to surrender or retreat. With more lorries available to move troops and tanks, he could also repeatedly shift the point of attack to keep the enemy off-balance. This all-arms approach quickly bore fruit, repelling the German spring offensives of 1918, then pushing the enemy back relentlessly through the late summer and autumn – at the cost of a further 235,000 French lives.

For the front-line soldier, however, large set-piece offensives were the exception.

More frequent were trench raids, ordered by staff officers avid for intelligence on enemy troop movements, while remaining comfortably immune from the inevitable retaliatory shelling. Prisoners were the aim, preferably men carrying their personal papers or badged with their regimental number. Four to ten men made up a raiding party – all volunteers – accompanied by a corporal or a sergeant and, if the occasion demanded, an officer. In some regiments these parties became a semi-permanent sub-unit, a *corps franc*.

Men killed in the front line were by necessity buried close at hand. In September 1915, at Perthes-lès-Hurlus (Marne), Jacques Arnoux (116th Infantry) spotted fragments of wooden crosses in the trench walls, all bearing partial inscriptions: 'Below a scrap of red kepi I read, "Here lie soldiers from 10th Infantry. Show your respect." Beside it, "Here lie fifteen brave men from 11th Infantry. Show your respect."' For the wounded, there was an established chain of evacuation and treatment. Casualties went first to a regimental aid post sited in the reserve trenches, or were collected and carried there by stretcher-bearers, normally the regimental bandsmen. The aid posts were simple dressing stations, where the regimental medical officer, assisted by an auxiliary (usually a medical student) and four medical orderlies, bandaged wounds and conducted an initial triage. From the aid post, those considered viable continued to one of several divisional field ambulances, where personal details were recorded and a further triage performed. Men with mortal or minor wounds remained in situ, while those judged suitable for further treatment were carried by the vehicles of the Motor Ambulance Units to Lines of Communication hospitals (HOE), situated some kilometres behind the lines.

Opposite top: Vauquois sector (Meuse), July 1915. The pre-war army had emphasized volume of fire over marksmanship, but the advent of trench warfare soon turned attention to sniping. Here, men in the front-line trenches use a sniperscope – one of a range of 'home-made' devices designed to allow a man to conceal himself when firing. The sniperscope, however, had one serious flaw: working the bolt required the shooter to manhandle down the whole frame, so revealing his position. Nor would every soldier would happily shoot the enemy in cold blood. Paul Tuffrau (246th Infantry) observed the reaction of two territorials when a German soldier showed himself in the trenches opposite. '"Go on, fire," ordered one. "I can't. He's too young," replied his chum. "Then give me your rifle," demanded the first. "No!" came the reply.'

Opposite below: Vauquois sector (Meuse), July 1915. The men of 31st Infantry occupy a sandbagged post in the front line, just 15m from the enemy. Léon Vuillermoz (44th Infantry) found himself in a similarly exposed position: 'We had little to fear apart from surprise attacks. We surrounded the crater with barbed wire, then tied tin cans to it, which would make a noise in response to any kind of movement.'

Post C, Les Éparges sector (Meuse). Two boxes of hand grenades lie ready to repel an attack on this outpost, with the Germans just 20m away. According to Sergeant Marc Bloch (272nd Infantry), it was hard to distinguish an enemy approach from 'the noises that make up the normal murmur of the night: the "tap, tap" of raindrops on foliage, so like the drumbeat of distant footsteps, the slightly metallic rustling sound of very dry leaves falling on ground already thick with them, often mistaken by the men for a German fitting a cartridge-clip into the breech of his gun.'

Ravin des Courtes-Chausses, near Montfaucon-en-Argonne (Meuse), July 1915. Lying between the French first and second lines in the wooded hills of the Argonne, the valley was the scene of heavy fighting during German attacks in the summer of 1915. Here, the entrance to a mine is pictured. Both armies used the skills of pre-war miners, and while the French dug towards the Germans, the enemy were coming in the opposite direction. 'The Germans set off a countermine,' Maurice Payen (409th Infantry, attached to 2nd Engineers) told his parents. 'We knew about their plans, so no one was working there. We blocked our tunnel with sandbags, so their mine, far from destroying it, turned it into a gun barrel that wrecked their own tunnel instead. We have to make them realise that miners from the Nord and Pas-de-Calais are just as canny as Westphalians.'

Ferme Confrécourt (Aisne), July 1916. Atrocious conditions faced the diggers. 'Next day I went to work shoring up the walls of the collapsed tunnel,' continued Payen. 'Five minutes later Lecomte was brought up, virtually suffocated... Five minutes later it was my go to be hauled out by the rope fixed to my belt, and so on and so forth... Turns about! As soon as we came round, we went back down again.'

Bois de Lachalade (Meuse), 23 September 1915. A mine explodes on Côte 285 during a local attack in support of the main Champagne offensive. One officer described the effects of an explosion beneath the German lines on the Aisne: 'At 3.30am we heard a dull thud and felt the ground shake beneath our feet. Then we saw – flung over 30 metres in the air by a huge explosion – an enormous mass of earth, stones, props, chevaux de frise and German bodies, including several that fell right up to our barbed wire.'

Le Labyrinthe, south of Neuville-Saint-Vaast (Pas-de-Calais), 25 September 1915. The joint Franco-British offensive in Artois was designed to divert German attention from the main French push in Champagne. Here, the French assault wave leaves its position to attack towards Vimy Ridge, just as the British were attacking at Loos (Pas-de-Calais). Both armies made inroads into the German positions but their attacks soon foundered – the French against machine guns sited deeper within enemy lines, as well as the difficult terrain of the ridge itself.

Bois de la Folie, west of Petit-Vimy (Pas-de-Calais), 25 September 1915. The men of III Corps advance into action against a background of smoke from the French flamethrowers. An officer from 28th Infantry described the operation of these terrible weapons: 'With a terrific whoosh, a jet of yellow liquid rises above P.40 [the French front-line trench]. The flamethrowers are going into action. Around every 30 metres, pieces of burning gel, tossed into the air by unseen hands, float toward the German trenches.'

Souain (Marne), 9.30am, 25 September 1915. The main French offensive in Champagne reached its apogee north of Souain and nearby Perthes-lès-Hurlus, but ground to a halt with heavy casualties before a succession of ridgelines held by the enemy. Here, the men of the third assault wave pause to catch their breath in the captured trenches of the German second line.

Ferme des Marquises, Prunay (Marne), July 1916. Machine-gunners from 114th Infantry operate a 1907-pattern Saint-Étienne in the trenches east of Reims. The Saint-Étienne, introduced into the army as a replacement for the 1897 Hotchkiss, proved inherently prone to overheating. Still, it remained in production until 1916 when it was finally replaced by the 1914 Hotchkiss.

Bombing school, Branscourt (Marne), September 1916. A gun-team struggles to manoeuvre a 37mm gun over broken ground. Introduced in May 1916 to units at Verdun and the Somme, the 37mm gun was supposed to provide close support during infantry attacks, but proved too cumbersome for its intended purpose. Although small, it was still very heavy, even when split into its three constituent parts: the shield (28kg), carried by the sergeant-commander; the tripod (38kg), by two numbers; and the barrel (48kg), by the gun layer and the loader.

Étang de Parroy sector (Meurthe-et-Moselle), January 1916. Two sentries observe German lines from firing steps in the trenches east of Nancy. The Lebel (left) is equipped with one of the recently introduced telescopic sights. These sights, designed to replace the locally produced sniperscopes, were fitted to rifles of proven accuracy and issued only to suitably qualified riflemen.

Les Éparges sector (Meuse), September 1916. Rather than the unwieldy 37mm gun, the French chose instead to equip teams with rifle-grenades. Here, the Lebels in this front-line battery have all been adapted to launch the Vivien-Bessières (VB) rifle-grenade – a 'bullet through' weapon fired using the standard cartridge. The grenade was placed in a special muzzle cup, the rifle butt set on the ground, and a bullet fired to strike the grenade and ignite an eight-second fuse. With a maximum range of 170m, the VB quickly became central to the new platoon tactics of 1916.

Côte de Chênois (Meuse), March 1917. Two men gaze over the moonscape of the shell-battered Verdun battlefield. On the horizon (left) is the Batterie de Damloup, which covered the south-eastern approaches to Fort Vaux. The position fell to the Germans on 3 July 1916 after its four 90mm guns had been destroyed by bombardment, but was recaptured by the French on 24 October 1916.

Training school, Third Army, Mouy (Oise), February 1917. The tactics developed for the 1916 Somme offensive emphasized the need for flexible formations, mutually supportive and capable of pressing deep into enemy positions, isolating strongpoints to be dealt with by the follow-up waves and trench-clearers. Here, the men undergoing assault training have adopted a mixed formation, with assault waves (in the background) flanked by columns.

General Robert Nivelle (1856–1924), Château d'Offémont (Oise), September 1915. Nivelle, then commander of 1st Infantry Division, is seen outside his HQ. Nivelle was an accomplished artillery commander whose unquenchable air of self-confidence propelled him from a regimental command in August 1914 to commander-in-chief in December 1916. Not everyone was convinced, however. 'Touchy, pushy, a military dilettante,' sniffed General Hubert Lyautey, the former French commander in Morocco briefly minister of war in the spring of 1917. And indeed Nivelle's fall, following the catastrophic failure of his Chemin des Dames offensive, was as meteoric as his rise.

General Charles Mangin (1866–1925), Regret (Marne), 9 November 1916. Mangin, then commander of XI Corps, consults a map outside his HQ with his chief of staff, Colonel Charles Fiévet. Mangin built a reputation as a thruster and, under the patronage of Nivelle, rose quickly to the command of Sixth Army in December 1916. He fell from favour alongside Nivelle, returning to an Army command in June 1918, and briefly commanding troops in the Army of Occupation before retiring in 1919. Fiévet was an artilleryman and experienced staff officer who died in 1919, worn out by his wartime exertions.

Champagne, September 1917. Trench-raiding teams, made up of the boldest and best, became a permanent feature in some regiments, although certain senior commanders, including Pétain, deplored such a concentration of talent. Here, trench raiders from 134th Infantry leave through the French wire on the heels of a supporting bombardment. Once the raiders reached their target, they would throw their grenades and enter the enemy trench – one party going left and one right. Bringing up the rear is a medical orderly.

Between Allemant and Pinon (Aisne), October 1917. French soldiers take possession of the enemy Giraffe Trench during the battle of La Malmaison at the western end of the Chemin des Dames ridge. German machine guns sited here had wreaked havoc on the attackers. The battle gained some 9.5km and 10,000 prisoners, at the cost of 2,241 French lives, also pulling in German reserves earmarked for imminent transfer to the Italian front. The strip of cloth lying across the trench serves to indicate the new French position to friendly aircraft.

Mont Cornillet sector, Monts-de-Champagne (Marne), 20 May 1917. The regimental stretcher-bearers gather themselves minutes before 1st Zouaves de marche launch their assault. A dreadful task awaited them, for the regiment lost 19 officers and 600 men in capturing the hill: 'Above it all hung an atmosphere heavy with dust, smoke, the acrid smell of explosives. Not to mention the raging thunder of guns and shells. Mont Cornillet truly was a corner of hell on the afternoon of 20 May.'

Mont Blond sector, Monts-de-Champagne (Marne), 20 May 1917. The German positions on Mont Blond covered those on Mont Cornillet further west; both heights were captured during the same offensive. Here, an officer fires a flare pistol from a trench captured during the attack. Aspirant Robert Ferat was one of those who took part: 'My platoon, composed largely of specialists (bombers, machine-gunners and sappers) was part of the first wave of the attack, which met no significant resistance and in a few hours advanced nearly 2km over ground bombarded for a week and covered in wood, iron and all kinds of debris. The task of my platoon was to neutralize any strongpoints capable of holding up the first and second waves. The moppers-up would deal with any prisoners. Many were already trapped in their comfortable shelters whose entrances had been partially blocked by our bombardment.'

General Henri Gouraud (1867–1946), Paris, May 1917. Gouraud had lost his right arm while commanding French troops at the Dardanelles in 1915, returning to duty as commander of Fourth Army within a matter of months. Colonel Douglas MacArthur was impressed by the man: 'With one arm gone, and half a leg missing, with his red beard glittering in the sunlight, the jaunty rake of his cocked hat and the oratorical brilliance of his resonant voice, his impact was overwhelming. He seemed almost to be the reincarnation of . . . Henry of Navarre. And he was just as good as he looked. I have known all of the modern French commanders, and many were great measured by any standards, but he was the greatest of them all.' Here, Gouraud (right), then Resident-General of Morocco, attends an exhibition of Moroccan art. He returned to the command of Fourth Army in the summer of 1917 and saw post-war service in Syria and Lebanon, both then French protectorates.

Marshal Ferdinand Foch (1851–1929), Château de Sarcus (Oise), May 1918. Foch, recently appointed Supreme Allied Commander on the Western Front, is pictured at his new HQ – his base until June 1918. Foch was another thruster, rising quickly from command of XX Corps in August 1914 to that of Northern Army Group. He was sacked early in 1917 in the wake of Joffre's dismissal, but returned rapidly to favour after the fall of Nivelle.

Near Chaudun (Aisne), 18 July 1918. A line of Senegalese tirailleurs occupy scrapes among the stubble. Some officers, notably General Mangin, saw Africa as a virtually inexhaustible reserve of manpower, and some 180,000 west Africans (termed Senegalese irrespective of their country of origin) joined the colours between 1914 and 1918. 'In the early days it was the whites who were always in the front line,' stated Kande Kamara, who served in France. 'But when we got to know them ... and they started to trust us ... things changed. By the end we were all mixed up ... and only the naive were frightened by colour. ... If we hadn't fought in western wars, travelled overseas and demonstrated our essential human dignity, black people would be completely disregarded today.'

Near Rivière (Pas-de-Calais), 1915. The German use of gas at Ypres in April 1915 occasioned a desperate search for adequate protection. Here, in the front-line trenches, Lieutenant du Bois Guehennec demonstrates an early pattern of gas mask, a commercial copy of the Dehoey-Leclercq. Although introduced into Fourth Army during the summer of 1915, the mask was rejected for general issue, the tightness of its elastic making it unadaptable to faces of different shape and size.

Bois des Zouaves, near Reims (Marne), October 1915. This soldier is wearing a Type P gas mask, another early pattern, introduced in August 1915. The Type P contained a pad made up of several layers of cloth impregnated with castor oil and ricinate soda, plus a separate pair of goggles. It gave some thirty minutes' protection against chlorine gas but was ineffective against phosgene.

Trench 15, Bois des Zouaves, near Reims (Marne), August 1915. Other anti-gas measures included the Vermorel sprayer, demonstrated here. Filled with a mixture of hyposulphite and sodium carbonate, it was effective against both chlorine and phosgene gases. In June 1917 the original mixture was replaced by a solution of sodium polysulphide, which also neutralized other poison gases. Concentrations in the soil were treated with lime chloride.

Main de Massiges sector, Ville-sur-Tourbe (Marne), December 1915. Clad in a sheepskin jerkin to ward off the fierce winter cold, this sentry wears a TN gas mask, which employed hyposulphite and protected against tear gas and phosgene. The TN remained in service throughout 1916 but was gradually replaced from April onwards by the M2, an improved version with integral goggles.

Apremont-le-Forêt (Meuse), May 1918. The men of a colonial regiment undergo gas-mask training. They are wearing the ARS mask, which was first adopted in January 1917 but only reached the lines in number the following year. The ARS used a new technology, adopting the German preference for a charcoal filter rather than the impregnated pad common to previous French patterns.

Sixth Army kennels, Septmonts (Aisne), April 1918. Even the army dogs received their own gas mask. Military kennels had first been established in 1913 at Toul (Meurthe-et-Moselle), using animals donated or loaned by private individuals. In 1915 a new Army Dogs Service was introduced to provide more systematic recruitment and training. Dogs were used in many roles: as couriers, watchdogs, ratters and guide dogs, as well as for light transport duties.

Cambligneul (Pas-de-Calais), May 1915. One attempt to provide mobile fire support was to fit a machine gun to a motor chassis. Here, a 1908 Clément-Bayard touring car sports a Saint-Étienne machine gun placed on a central mount. These modified vehicles were first used in Morocco in 1908, but proved unsuitable for unmade roads. Shipped back to France, they were attached to divisional or corps headquarters and used mainly to guard regimental transport columns. They rarely saw action, but the men of 60th Chasseurs had reason to be grateful for their help in escaping a tight corner near Bazoches (Aisne) in 1914.

Noyon (Oise), March 1917. Two Renault armoured cars pass through the Place de l'Hôtel de Ville, shortly after the Germans evacuated the town as part of a planned withdrawal to the more easily defended Hindenburg line. The first Renault armoured cars were produced in 1914, but they proved unsatisfactory, with inadequate armour and an ill-ventilated engine, and the following year they were replaced by this type, armed with either a machine gun or a 37mm gun. Seventeen armoured-car groups were formed in 1916 and attached to cavalry formations, but they saw little action until the final year of the conflict.

Courlandon (Marne), April 1917. The crew of the Schneider tank *Malèche* (2nd Battery, AS8) are seen here with their dog. The French first began to investigate tracked vehicles as a means of crossing broken ground under protection in 1915, and the pioneering Schneider was delivered in September 1916. Each tank was routinely named by its crew; here, *Malèche* ('Never mind') is painted on the side in French and Arabic. The driver peers through his viewing port, while the dog has the best seat in the house. Tank crews welcomed dogs for their companionship, but also for their greater sensitivity to any build-up of carbon monoxide, one of the many flaws besetting early models.

Condé-sur-Aisne (Aisne), 3 May 1917. The newly delivered Saint-Chamond tanks of AS31 pass through the village. The Saint-Chamond was the second French heavy tank of the war, developed as a commercial rival to the Schneider, the first examples leaving the factory in April 1917. Over 5/6 May 1917 the Groupement Lefèvre – two groups of Saint-Chamonds and two of Schneiders, plus accompanying infantry – forced a breach in the German lines at the Moulin de Laffaux (Aisne): 'rutted, churned and scorched by the artillery preparation, the ground wasn't firm but a sort of crumbling, shifting ash, full of adjoining shell-holes that gave way beneath our tracks'.

Condé-sur-Aisne (Aisne), 3 May 1917. Lieutenant Bégarie, CO of 1st Battery, AS31, and commander of the Saint-Chamond *Teddy*, is just visible here (in beret) in the hatch (right). Standing on the tank is the unit CO, Captain Calumels. The tank was named after the toy bear owned by Bégarie's son and later became an instructional frame for AS Group XII (AS37/38/39).

Tank school, near Marly-le-Roi (Yvelines), 1916. The positions of the driver (left) and gunner (right) are shown inside the cramped interior of the Saint-Chamond. The gun was a modified 75mm field gun; the gunner sat left of the breech, with the ammunition placed in the rack to his rear. The armament was completed by two machine guns – one on either side of the tank. But so tight was the available space that one machine-gunner had to straddle the trail of the 75 to operate his weapon.

Bois de Sénécat (Somme), 18 April 1918. Sous-lieutenant Decrette (1st Battery, AS3), commander of the Schneider *Mets-z'y-en* ('Get stuck in'), checks his tank for damage after an attack on the wood. The appliqué armour plate had done its job: none of the German armour-piercing bullets had penetrated the hull. Two months later Henri Desagneux (359th Infantry) watched another group of Saint-Chamonds come under attack: 'Suddenly we heard a shout, "Tanks!" Big Saint-Chamonds. Off they went, huge monsters advancing down the road in broad daylight. Quite a sight! The Boches concentrated all their guns upon them; shells rained down. Several tanks were destroyed in situ, some were ablaze, some staggered on in search of flat ground but were soon bogged down, some got across the German trenches only to be wiped out within 100m. Fifteen minutes later it was all over. Today will have cost us thirty-seven of the forty tanks supporting the division.'

Near Épernay (Marne), 2 June 1918. A Renault tank is loaded on a heavy trailer for transport by road. Unlike the cumbersome Schneiders and Saint-Chamonds, the Renault FT – developed by Louis Renault in the face of official reluctance – was a light tank, weighing only 6t and with a top speed of 12km/h. Carried by lorry, or on one of a range of heavy trailers manufactured by companies like La Buire or Boilot-Pétolat, it could be concentrated quickly and deployed in support of offensives or counter-attacks.

Oulchy-le-Château (Aisne), 30 July 1918. A trio of camouflaged Renault FT light tanks is pictured here in the ruined village. The tank (left) is armed with a machine gun, but its companions, including *Sans Pitié* ('Merciless'), both carry a 37mm gun. Oulchy was an island of enemy resistance during the second battle of the Marne, eventually falling on 25 July 1918 to an attack from front and rear by regiments of 41st Division.

Tank school, Champlieu (Oise), July 1917. The Renault FT only required a two-man crew, a significant advantage when the French were beginning to run short of men. But it offered almost no internal space: the gunner/commander had to stand or sit on an extemporized leather strap in the turret, conveying his instructions by kicking the driver. Here, the man on the right has swapped his boots for pattens as protection against the mud, while the helmet resting on the track bears the crossed-gun badge of the artillery.

Camp de Clairs Chênes, near Dombasle-en-Argonne (Meuse), September 1918. Renault FT tanks undergo a final mechanical check before taking part in the successful attack launched by five light tank battalions and two heavy tank groups at Montfaucon (Meuse) on 26 September. The FT was plagued by radiator problems, and its engine, radiator, gears and fuel tank could only be accessed from the outside. 'The Renault tank', commented one cynic, 'is a machine that has by definition broken down but nonetheless deigns to work occasionally!'

Near Mont de Laffaux (Aisne), 23 October 1917. A wounded Senegalese soldier is sent to the rear during the battle of La Malmaison. Seventeen battalions of west Africans took part in the doomed April 1917 offensive on the Chemin des Dames ridge, and 43rd Bataillon de Tirailleurs Sénégalais returned in October to become the first west African unit decorated for gallantry with the lanyard in the colours of the Croix de guerre. Of the 180,000 west Africans who joined the colours during the course of the conflict, some 25,000 were killed.

Neuville-Saint-Vaast (Pas-de-Calais), 22 May 1915. A preliminary dressing is applied at a regimental aid post. The French had taken this village between Arras and Lens after heavy fighting earlier that month and were now engaged in repelling a series of determined but unsuccessful German counter-attacks.

Near Laffaux (Aisne), 16 April 1917. Sheltered by a railway embankment, wounded men are bandaged at an aid post on the opening day of the Chemin des Dames offensive. A soldier from 89th Infantry witnessed a similar scene: 'From then on the crowd of wounded grew relentlessly. They came in small groups, in whole companies, besieging the aid post – stooping, muddy, wretched, groaning. Some were drenched in blood, with just handkerchiefs or rags to cover their wounds. They showed us their injuries, their burns, their pierced and swollen flesh ... their terrible faces! Poor souls arrived on stretchers – without feet, without hands, howling like beasts. Soon the aid post was full, full to bursting, and still they came – more human wrecks, more bloody monsters.'

Between Concevreux and Maizy (Aisne), April 1917. Exhausted medical personnel snatch a brief rest on the banks of the Canal Latéral de l'Aisne. Lucien Laby (294th Infantry) served at Verdun in 1916: knew how tired they were. 'The wounded swamped our aid post. We dressed their wounds non-stop, communicating only by sign language. Talking was impossible, we couldn't hear ourselves speak.... Flesh wounds or grievous injuries, I worked flat out to do what I could for them all. I also tended to stretcher cases left outside the aid post, which soon wasn't big enough to admit everyone.'

Soupir (Marne), 17 April 1917. German prisoners were also used as stretcher-bearers. Here, a man is about to be evacuated from an aid post for further care and triage at a field ambulance. Charles Leleux, serving with a XXI Corps field ambulance, described the procedure awaiting him: 'Before tending [the wounded], first we have to clear away the mud and cut off their horrible wet clothes – a task performed admirably by our dedicated medical orderlies. They are a pleasure to behold, working so methodically, each man at his post. A new arrival is laid on the treatment table. While the orderlies prepare the instruments and expose his wound, a "writer" approaches him, locates his identity disk, asks for his regiment, company and rank, and notes it all in the admissions register. Then once the poor lad has been washed, treated and swathed in white linen, another pen-pusher – as the men like to call them – pins to his chest the diagnosis card that determines where he goes next.'

Ferme d'Offémont (Oise), June 1915. A group of wounded men is pictured with staff of Ambulance 4/37, one of the five field ambulances serving with 37th Infantry Division. The regiments that made up the division's infantry component were all raised in north Africa, among them 2nd Zouaves de marche. After suffering heavy losses over the previous winter, 2nd Zouaves were then engaged in attempts to pinch out a salient in the enemy lines. The attackers met with early success, but the German artillery forced the majority to withdraw over the next ten days, at a cost to the regiment of 25 officers and 1,250 men. Serving with 2nd Zouaves was Father Édouard (fourth left). The priest was decorated for bravery during the attack at Quennevières (Oise) on 6 June, but died later that year in Champagne.

Beaurieux (Aisne), 1917. A Charron motor ambulance evacuates men wounded during the attack on Craonne. 'We evacuated men judged capable of hanging on for treatment further to the rear,' recalled a member of Ambulance 9/3. 'But as soon they heard the engine throbbing, they wanted to be off. We saw men begging to be evacuated, entering their death throes even while insisting they were fit enough to travel. Some talked about themselves; most were silent. They wanted to be elsewhere... and above of all to sleep and have something to drink. Normal bodily functions asserted themselves, masking the pain from their wounds. I remember one poor fellow who was asked if he wanted anything... He was waiting for a serious chest wound to be examined. He whispered that he wanted to pass water. But by the time the orderly rushed back with a bottle, the man was dead.'

Chapter Three

'Warriors ready for anything'

For the front-line soldier, battle – whether large-scale offensive or trench raid – remained the exception. Watches, patrols and construction work made up his daily round. 'Torn from family, home and job, the French citizen is from one day to the next a warrior, ready for anything, a builder, an engineer, a bricklayer, a marksman, a bomber, a machine gunner or a cook,' wrote a man from 227th Infantry in 1915. By day, one quarter of any unit was occupied on sentry duty, and by night, one half was standing guard in two-hour watches. Meanwhile working parties laboured round the clock: in daylight there were old trenches to repair, new ones to dig, gabions to make and fill, supplies – wire, sandbags, ammunition – to fetch from the reserve lines. At night, men worked out in no man's land, repairing the barbed wire and, in the early days at least, clearing long grass; stretcher-bearers ventured out to retrieve the wounded; details departed to bring up food and water.

Many dugouts, particularly in the front line, were simply 'funk holes' scraped into one wall of the trench. Philippe Barrès, serving with the dismounted 12th Cuirassiers, offered this advice to the prospective winter resident: 'Don't stick your legs outside your scrape, it's raining. Don't lift your eyes or the rain will get in. Don't wiggle your arms or icy water will run beneath your blanket . . . but remember to move or you'll freeze. And don't fall asleep.' In sectors where timber was available, more permanent dugouts were constructed, employing a tent section to catch the water; on the reverse slopes of the rocky Vosges mountains, soldiers built small wooden sleeping huts; in the chalk of the Vauquois, they burrowed. 'Steps descended 15m below ground level, with bunk beds occupying half their width,' wrote André Pézard (46th Infantry). 'It was our dormitory, sitting room and dining hall. Whatever its occupants lacked in ventilation, they gained in security.'

Fatigued by working parties, and with normal sleep patterns disrupted by sentry duty and bombardments, soldiers learned to nap at any time. One man soon discovered 'how to sleep in wet boots because once you took them off you couldn't get them back on again. How to snooze for four hours in a sodden greatcoat, amid the explosions, shouts and stench.' But sometimes slumber was impossible, as Charles Delvert (101st Infantry) discovered in the trenches at Verdun: 'We can't get a moment's rest. The fleas are devouring us. Even when we're not under fire, we can feel them biting. On Saturday I noted in my diary that I hadn't slept for seventy-two hours.' To some wags, the fleas deserved the Iron Cross for their contribution to the German war effort.

Nor were fleas the only problem; the soldiers were also plagued by rats. 'Rats, rats beyond measure, are the true masters of the position,' claimed Jacques Vandebeuque (56th Chasseurs), serving in front of Les Éparges (Meuse). 'They multiply by their hundreds in every ruined house, every dugout ... I've spent terrible nights wrapped in my galoshes and greatcoat, aware of these dreadful beasts gnawing away at me. They outnumber us by fifteen or twenty to one; they eat all the bread, butter and chocolate, then start on our clothes. Sleep is impossible in these conditions. I throw off my blanket a hundred times a night and scare them away with a light, but the relief is short lived. They return almost immediately, more numerous than ever.'

To alleviate the soldiers' misery, family and friends sent parcels filled with all manner of items – including knitted gloves and scarves in a riot of colours, books and tobacco. Food, often home-grown or home-made, was particularly welcome. By an unspoken rule, it was shared between all the members of a section and made a welcome supplement to the rations. For men with no family, or southerners far from home, a female pen pal (*marraine de guerre*) offered an element of human warmth, an evocation of peacetime normality, completely absent from the front line. Some relationships prospered and were made permanent after the war; others were more transitory, but nevertheless provided a reliable source of material comforts.

Food parcels apart, men depended for their nourishment on the company cooks. The main meal of the day was scheduled at 10.00am for other ranks, 10.30am for NCOs and 11.00am for officers. The colonel ate at noon, and generals often later still. But this timetable was frequently ignored – during a relief, for example, or a more permanent move, and especially during attacks. 'We ate whenever we had the chance in case we couldn't eat when we wanted,' confessed one man. Each company was equipped with mobile cookers stationed in the second line of trenches or even further to the rear, so all hot food had to be carried to the front line – often a perilous task. At Verdun a party from 18th Chasseurs took all night to regain their positions: 'they returned at dawn, bone weary, covering the last hundred yards under enemy machine-gun fire. They were completely drained, claiming they would rather starve than repeat the exercise; but that evening, driven by an ingrained sense of duty and comradeship, they set out once more across the cratered ground.'

Two ration scales were in operation, depending on a regiment's current activities: both included 700g of bread, 600g of fresh meat and 300g of tinned meat daily, plus 50cl of wine, or a litre of beer or cider, or 6.25cl of spirits; the higher scale was distinguished mainly by an extra dole of potatoes, pasta, sugar and coffee. Tinned sardines in oil often replaced the meat, while rations for Muslim regiments excluded pork and alcohol. Every regiment also kept several days' reserve of preserved food: canned, stringy beef in gravy ('monkey'), a dozen pieces of hardtack per man, coffee tablets, packets of sugar and dried soup. Each company also received a small stipend, administered by the sergent-major (the NCO in charge of administration), to spend on local produce where available. Cooperatives, too, were established in some rear areas, allowing soldiers to buy their own extras.

Some men appreciated the company cooks and their efforts to produce meals under trying circumstances. Others, like Lieutenant Jacques Meyer (329th Infantry), were rather less grateful: 'The main meal of the day, called "soup" regardless, consisted of meat accompanied by a lump of rubbery pasta or rice, or by beans, more or less cooked, or potatoes, more or less peeled, all swimming in a brown liquid, and scarcely distinguishable under a surface layer of congealing fat. Greens were out of the question. Vitamins, too.'

To wash it all down came milky, well-sugared coffee and red wine. If mud loomed large in a soldier's life by necessity, wine – *pinard* – did so by choice. It was only simple *vin ordinaire*, and the company cooks were always under suspicion of watering it down, yet still it provided a real boost to morale: 'Water, the ordinary drink of the soldier; wine, the extraordinary,' claimed one trench newspaper. Many a battalion at rest contrived to secure extra supplies, finding a pretext to send a party armed with twenty or thirty water bottles to top up in a nearby village. Canny soldiers took care to fire a preliminary blank into the bottle, using the gases discharged to increase its normal 2l capacity. Before an attack, or in extremely cold weather, a rough eau-de-vie (*gnôle*) might also be distributed at the rate of 12.5cl per section. Doling out the wine and spirits was the job of the corporal, who was expected to provide fair shares every time – however many men were present.

Opposite below: Near Fort Regret, south-west of Verdun (Meuse), June 1916. Columns of infantrymen march from the railhead towards the front. Fort Regret covered the approach to the city from Bar-le-Duc; it was safe from serious shelling and became an important depot and staging post for soldiers entering and leaving the front line. The men of 151st Infantry passed this way in February 1916: 'we spotted the battlefield to the north, therefore to our left. It was lit up sporadically by shell-bursts, flares and even more ominously by the burning villages and farms. Huge shells were falling, sporadically, on Verdun.'

Clermont-en-Argonne (Meuse), July 1915. Soldiers entering the trenches covered the final stretch of the journey on foot. Here, an infantry column marches east through the rain down Rue Thiers. The Germans had occupied Clermont briefly in September 1914 and torched it when they withdrew. Visiting shortly afterwards, journalist René Dubreuil thought the village a necropolis, but on his return in December 1915 signs of life were evident once more: 'To my surprise, I could see from a distance plumes of smoke rising from the ruins. . . . At every turn I encountered new houses sheltering the old inhabitants. They are only modest wooden shacks erected among the ruins and charred masonry, nothing sumptuous. But in these simple homes life resumes happily enough. The birds are back in their nests.'

Near Chassemy (Aisne), November 1914. The men of 43rd Infantry occupy an early trench. Digging these first trenches was a very ad hoc affair, reported Corporal Louis Barthas (280th Infantry). Barthas was carrying an entrenching tool strapped to his pack, while his companion had a pick: 'With these two tools, lying prone, and after long and repeated efforts, we finally raised a low earthen bank as protection. Our neighbours in the adjoining holes were doing likewise, and we managed to link up to form a shallow trench, from where we could at last thumb our noses at the Kaiser's machine-gunners.'

Hartmannswillerkopf (Haut-Rhin), March 1916. Chasseurs à pied occupy an unimproved trench on the Vosges front. In this mountainous region the soil was too thin for deep trenches, forcing men to pile up stones for protection. 'I don't know when we'll be relieved,' complained chasseur officer Ferdinand Belmont (11th Chasseurs Alpins). 'The men are in tatters, their boots split, the state of their trousers more worrying still. Washing is out of the question. They haven't had a change of linen for a month. When it's not too cold they amuse themselves hunting for lice. But morale is high: neither filth, vermin nor rain can dampen their spirits.'

Near Vic-sur-Aisne (Aisne), 1915. French commanders were still expecting an early resumption of the war of movement, so this trench has been improved with wicker trench supports – easy and cheap to construct and repair. Typically for the period, the men holding the front line are wearing a mixture of pre-war and wartime uniform. Horizon blue uniforms were introduced in theory at the start of the war, but production delays had slowed their distribution. To economize on materials and expedite supply, the double-breasted greatcoat was changed to single-breasted, and the number of pockets reduced. As an interim measure, soldiers were also issued with dark blue or brown tunics and trousers in various materials, including corduroy. The NCO (centre) appears to be wearing his pre-war tunic, and all are wearing pre-war gaiters rather than puttees.

Near Saint-Thomas-en-Argonne (Marne), July 1915. This shallow trench is protected by a wall of gabions, a feature of field fortifications since medieval times. The wicker baskets were light to transport and simple to manufacture. Filled with earth, they weighed 18–22kg and created a sound, easily repairable barrier. One man (second left) holds his white-metal mess-tin. 'The Germans bronzed their mess-tins,' recalled Captain Charles Delvert. 'A seemingly minor point. Wrong, a very important detail. How many reliefs were wiped out, betrayed by their gleaming mess-tins?'

Vendresse-et-Troyon (Aisne), July 1916. The French front-line trenches close to the quarries at Ardussec are defended by barbed wire. According to official instructions dated 1917, wire was 'the best form of ancillary defence', easily erected over large swathes of ground. It was not wholly immune to gunfire, but effecting a practicable breach required huge quantities of ammunition: 500 artillery rounds or 3,000 machine-gun rounds. 'By rendering a position impregnable, barbed wire is the most important factor in this war,' thought Captain Charles Delvert. 'One lone sniper behind an intact, or virtually intact, entanglement can stop a half-platoon. And to think how ignorant we were of [it] before the war. . . . The better we protect men, the better they fight.'

Xivray (Meuse), 1917. The extreme narrowness of many trenches caused real problems, as Adjudant Zacharie Baqué (288th Infantry) discovered en route to his front-line position: 'You can imagine the bumps, bashed noses and blockages in a *boyau* [communication trench] just 80cm wide when a hundred men, all fully laden, meet a working party coming out – equal in size, and no less burdened with empty shell cases, cauldrons, cooking vessels and the like.'

Vauquois (Meuse), July 1915. Men repair a position in the village. At the Main de Massiges in March 1916, Charles Delvert described the work involved: 'My soldiers are a fine bunch of lads. As soon as their watch is over, they grab their picks and shovels. They dig and clear the trenches, reinforcing the walls with iron posts and wire mesh, and constructing protective berms wherever possible. They create firing steps from all kinds of material: crates, sandbags, wire mesh, planks laid lengthwise and supported by stakes. Solid splinter-proofs enclosed by chicken wire and reinforced with wooden stakes 1.5–2m long present a rounded profile. Meanwhile other men are excavating saps, positioning framework, uprights and caps, erecting timber cladding . . .'

Near Bois Chauffour (Oise), 10 April 1918. *Bouasse, boue, bouillasse, cafouille, pastiss, patouille* – military slang for just one thing: mud. Here, men from 47th Infantry struggle down a trench on Côte 259. Emerging from the front line at Verdun in July 1916, Charles Delvert and his men endured 'an interminable trek through the darkness via Côte 181. We marched nose to tail through clinging mud for five long hours, slipping with every step, sometimes disappearing up to our knees. No marked path, fatigue compounded by uncertainty. Endless halts because the men were no longer following. Unsure where we were putting our feet. Visibility down to 5m. [Then] the shells started bursting all around us.'

Near Bourg-et-Comin (Aisne), July 1916. Many French communication trenches were allowed to become overgrown. 'The sodden grass dangling into the *boyaux* whips you in the face,' complained Delvert at the Main de Massiges in July 1916. However, the vegetation could have its uses: using a hare shot by one of his comrades, Albert Lamaignerie (142nd Territorials) 'made an excellent civet with summer herbs from the trench. Fried eggs, pancakes, the saddle beautifully cooked. Delicious.'

Near Chivy (Aisne), August 1917. Men from a working party, carrying duckboards into the front line, stop to take a breather. Duckboards were normally used to allow passage along the muddy trenches, but sometimes the need was more general. Paul Clerfeuille (273rd Infantry) was serving on the Chemin des Dames in 1918: 'We are positioned in a swamp in the Bois de Beau Marais. The water gets everywhere, even our cement and corrugated-iron dugouts. We've got to lay duckboards all over. There are wild ducks nesting in the reeds.'

Neuville-Saint-Vaast (Pas-de-Calais), 23 May 1915. French troops try to settle into a recently captured trench. 'A sap?' enquired *Le Filon*, the trench newspaper of 83rd Infantry, 'a sumptuous luxury known only in quiet sectors ... Elsewhere we sleep wrapped in a tent section, curled up in a niche in the trench wall ... [or out] under the stars ... in the shell-holes ... when they're not flooded or full of snow ... [where] your limbs stiffen and shiver ... your heart too, where your feet are encased in frozen mud.'

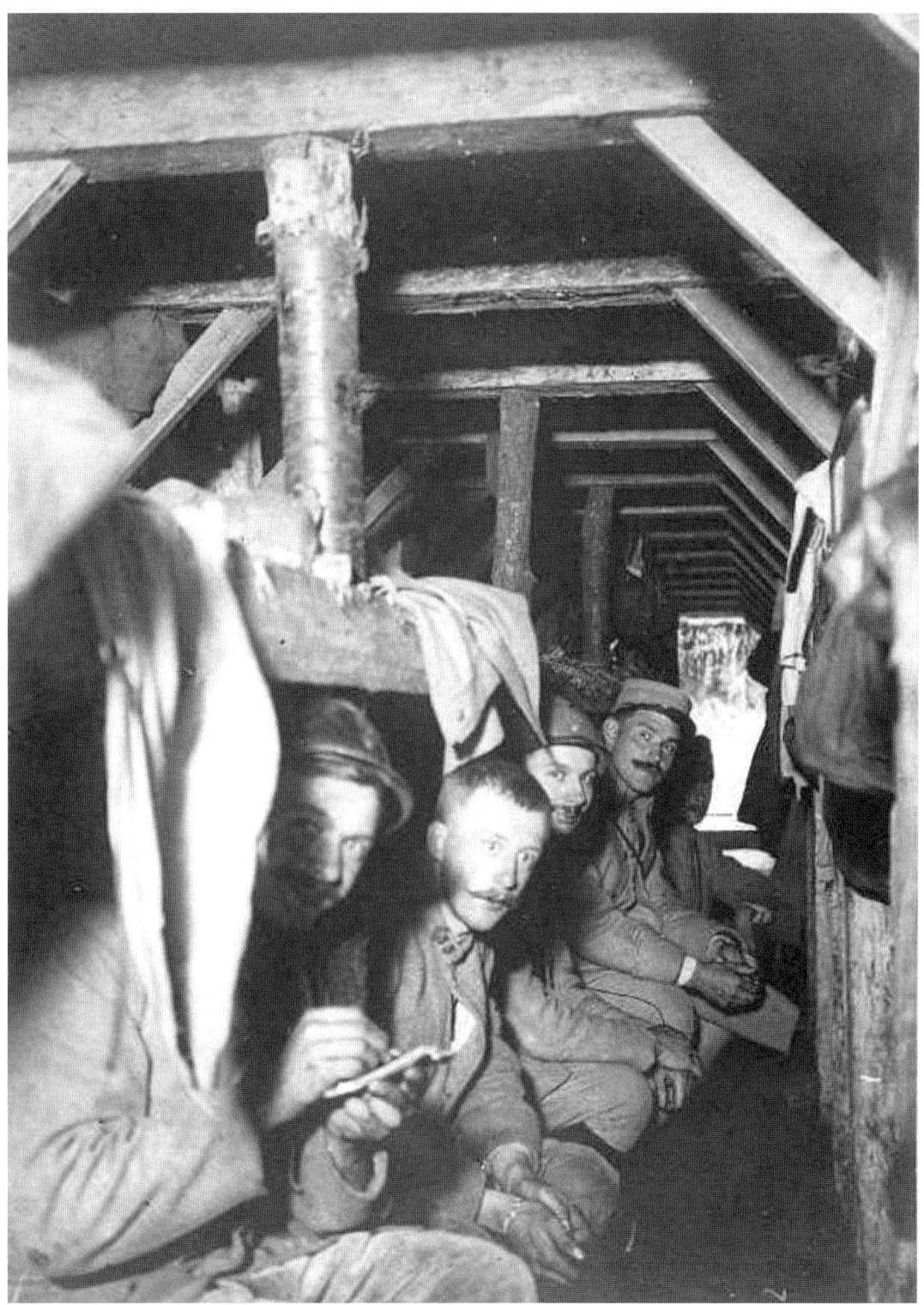

Verneuil-Courtonne sector (Aisne), July 1916. There is precious little headroom in this dugout occupied by 33rd Infantry. Situated in the line between the Aisne and the Chemin des Dames, it was designed to accommodate a company of about 200 men. Both Verneuil and the adjoining Moussy-sur-Aisne were destroyed in the fighting; the villages were later rebuilt and combined in 1923 as the modern commune of Moussy-Verneuil.

Oulches (Aisne), August 1915. Their equipment hanging from hooks in the wall, men snatch some rest in this cramped cellar billet. Albert Thierry (28th Infantry) suffered in similar conditions. His billet, he reported, was 'a ghastly sardine tin where eleven of us lie soaking on a bed of muddy straw'.

Near Bétheny (Marne), February 1918. Lieutenant Colonel Octave Meynier (1st Tirailleurs de marche) and his staff enjoy rather more salubrious surroundings in the mess of their HQ dugout. Meynier (seated, third from left), a veteran of action in west and north Africa, took command of his regiment in May 1917. He would lose his left arm in action eleven months later.

Near Soissons (Aisne), August 1916. Runners gather in a brigade HQ dugout in the Saint-Paul salient. Behind them a poster bears Pétain's defiant call to arms: ON LES AURAS (sic)/'We'll have 'em'. Charles Delvert greatly admired his runner Bocage: 'Cool under shelling, funny and brave. He would reach the dugout out of breath after running through the barrage, collapse on the bottom step and fan himself with his helmet: "Those pigs don't have a clue."'

Near Hurtebise (Aisne), July 1917. A rations party brings hot food to the front lines. 'You don't just think about food while you're asleep,' claimed Étienne Tanty (129th Infantry). 'Better still, in my case anyway... I'm always eating. It's strange. I dream about bread, sitting at the table, and food of all kinds. I devour the poached pears and *gateaux de riz* my mother used to make... or... I go and sniff the crust of the pies in Eugénie's oven.'

Near Hartmannswillerkopf (Haut-Rhin), October 1916. A rations party of machine-gunners from 245th Infantry trudges uphill near Camp Renié. Sylvain Wannenmacher (109th Infantry) describes how such teams were organized: 'One man for the bread loaves, strung like a rosary from a piece of wire and wrapped across the chest; another for the water-bottles previously handed over by each man in his section, now filled with coffee and *pinard*. . . . Finally, a man with the '*boutehous*' [lidded pails for hot food]. They make up a caravan which sets off by night for the rear, to a pre-arranged spot where the mobile cookers come to meet them. They return laden like donkeys, heads bowed to support the burden cutting into their shoulders.'

Bois des Buttes (Aisne), September 1917. Mealtime for the men of 204th Infantry. 'We've been fed no better than swine for the past few days,' Lucien Papillon (174th Infantry) complained to his parents. 'Rice twice a day, wine [375cl]; I think we're running short of rations. Spuds are completely off the menu.'

Near Badonviller (Meurthe-et-Moselle), September 1915. The men of 358th Infantry enjoy a moment of relaxation in the front line, manufacturing souvenirs from shell fragments. '[We make] things to please all the mothers, sisters, fiancées and sweethearts in the rear!' reported Émile Morin (42nd Infantry). 'We use whatever is to hand: a few files, a little saw – often made from a spring, a small hammer perhaps, and a good knife. Armed with these rudimentary tools, the poilus patiently saw, trim, file, scrub and polish for hours on end, sitting on the firing step or outside the dugout.'

Camp Renié, Hartmannswillerkopf (Haut-Rhin), March 1916. Two extravagantly moustachioed officers from 53rd Infantry enjoy a rest period at this camp in the Bois de Wattwiller, just south of the modern Hartmannswillerkopf National Cemetery. The French created several such camps amid the pine forests of the Vosges mountains, immediately behind the trenches. They provided rest facilities for front-line troops, sparing them a tortuous descent to the valleys below.

Saint-Thomas-en-Argonne (Marne), 25 July 1915. Resting on a copy of *Le Petit Parisien*, a popular national daily, a Provençal from 255th Infantry writes a letter. He wears a neckerchief and temporary-issue corduroy trousers, as well as a metal skull-cap to protect his head. The cap was issued in February 1915 to be worn underneath the kepi. However, it was uncomfortable and unventilated and, like many of his comrades, this man prefers to leave it on top.

Near Sapicourt (Marne), September 1916. A trench mortar section marches along the Courcelles road, the men unable to hide their joy at escaping the front line. The fiddler (centre) plays a tune, while his chums sing along. Serving in the trenches alongside the infantry, Engineer Lieutenant Gueneau (20/2 Field Company) knew the same emotion: 'The relief! The relief! It's so good to be alive. We pass more infantrymen, also coming out of the trenches, awful to behold in their carapace of mud. How glory is defiled. One man, fully laden, slips and measures his length, almost disappearing in a ditch full of gluey mud. He picks himself up, laughing and waving, scarcely any filthier than before. He couldn't care less. It's the relief!'

Chapter Four

'We know nothing of glory'

An enormous gulf separated new recruit and veteran, and men had to adapt quickly on reaching their new unit. The arrival of 'three dazed newcomers' is described by author Roland Dorgelès (39th Infantry) in his novel *Les Croix de bois*: 'We were on our feet and formed an inquisitive circle around [them]. They looked at us. We looked at them. Nobody spoke. They'd just come from the rear. Only yesterday they were walking the city streets, seeing women, trams, shops. Only yesterday they were living like men. We stood transfixed, regarding them with envy. They were voyagers from a far-off land.'

Blending these newcomers into a fighting unit was the task of junior officers and NCOs (in the French army those ranked sergeant and above), but unofficially each man in the section lent a hand. Front-line combat demanded a high degree of mutual support and, for Captain Charles Delvert (101st Infantry), men 'would feel like cowards if they flinched'. When a comrade of Louis Barthas (280th Infantry) suffered a leg wound that later led to amputation, he was rebuked by his comrades for making a fuss: 'we teased him for carrying on like a sissy,' recalled Barthas. Buoyed by this solidarity, some units and formations had a particular reputation for bravery. With their pre-war prestige and campaign experience, the colonial infantry and north African regiments – the zouaves and the tirailleurs – were widely regarded as elite assault troops, even after heavy casualties had reduced many to a standard no better than ordinary line infantry. Most distinguished of all was perhaps the Régiment d'Infanterie Coloniale du Maroc, which was created from a number of battalions serving in Morocco in August 1914. The RICM became a formidable unit, its number of citations demanding the creation of a new distinction, the double lanyard of the Croix de guerre, to reward the outstanding courage of its men.

Mutual support within the section was not confined to battle: letters, parcels and news from home were all shared between its members. NCOs too could sympathize with their men. Sergeant Marc Bloch (272nd Infantry) recalled a sergeant doing 'his utmost to make life more agreeable for those of his men he thought were hard up, sharing those little comforts that are so prized on campaign.

He had a very lofty notion of camaraderie.' Meanwhile if an NCO was officious or overbearing, his men could soon find ways to make their resentment felt: for example, Louis Barthas' section ostracized their sergeant for reporting one man's casual grumbling to the company commander.

As far as officers were concerned, private soldiers reserved some of their highest praise for the 'good father', who looked after them and refused to fritter their lives away. The good officer was also prepared to share the same risks as his troops. 'Our lieutenant set the example, so we were happy to follow,' claimed Frédéric Charignon (75th Infantry). But not all officers were as willing to put themselves in harm's way. Sergeant Jean Bec (122nd Infantry) chided those 'afraid to go outside and do their business. They use an empty can and leave the orderly to dispose of it over the parapet.'

Good or bad, there was always a distance between leader and led. Officers messed together, as did NCOs. 'The officers discuss women; the NCOs, pensions and promotion; and the soldiers, wine,' commented Pierre Chaine (351st Infantry). 'But love is rare, wine expensive, and promotions scarce.' The difference between ranks was also made explicit in matters of hygiene, with signs identifying 'lavatories for the officers, toilets for the NCOs and latrines for the men'. Senior officers in particular were remote figures. The leader of any unsuccessful operation was quickly castigated as a 'butcher' or 'bloodsucker', while Sous-lieutenant Abel Ferry (166th Infantry) claimed the men of his company could name only two officers – the company commander and General Joffre. Just a handful of senior officers acquired a good reputation during the conflict, notably Pétain and Gouraud. In 1921, however, Castelnau, Gouraud, Mangin, Maunoury, Degoutte and Nivelle topped a newspaper poll to rank a list of generals for possible promotion to a marshalcy, each attracting over 4 million votes. In the event, only Maunoury was so honoured – and that, posthumously.

The men of 1914 had marched to war with enthusiasm, to drive out the invader and liberate the 'lost provinces' of Alsace and Lorraine, but attitudes changed over the first months of the conflict, replaced by a grim determination to see it through. In 1914 senior commanders expected pacifist propaganda to have a profound impact on the numbers answering the call-up. In the event, despite the huge scale of French losses, men continued to comply with the summons: just under 1 per cent of conscripts failed to appear in 1918, substantially fewer than the 2.6 per cent recorded in 1915. 'The soldier of 1916 fights not for Alsace, nor to ruin Germany, nor for his country,' opined Second Lieutenant Louis Mairet (127th Infantry), two days into the Somme offensive. 'He fights out of decency, habit and necessity. He fights because he has no alternative.' Ideas of glory, *la gloire*, much cited by the press, were dismissed out of hand. 'Glory spurns the attentions of mudlarks like us,' wrote

Major Jean Henches (32nd Artillery). 'We know nothing of her; she knows nothing of us. We ask nothing of her; she promises us nothing.'

For Pierre Chaine, front-line soldiers passed through a number of stages. 'First comes that of the recruit yet to endure his baptism of fire, a time of waiting and frayed nerves. The soldier is prey to all kinds of wild imaginings, his initiation both longed for and dreaded. Then, after emerging unscathed from several engagements, he loses his fear of fire for a time. He starts to believe that the shells will not touch him, the bullets will always whistle by. . . . Eventually, however, his good luck makes him edgy. The odds seem to be narrowing all the time. He hates having to place another bet after every winning gamble. . . . [But] soldiers are only truly battle hardened at the fourth stage, when they no longer care about their own survival, even preferring a swift end to their daily joust with death.' The modern form of bravery, he concluded, was to stand firm before an invisible and inevitable demise.

Yet not every recruit acquiesced readily to a life under military discipline. Desertion and self-inflicted wounds were common, and in September 1914 normal court martial procedures were suspended and replaced by a system of summary tribunals. Sentences were carried out within twenty-four hours, with no right of appeal, and over a two-day period in October 1914 Fourth Army condemned thirty-one men to death for self-inflicted wounds, executing thirteen by firing squad: Lucien Bersot (60th Infantry), for example, was shot for refusing to don a pair of trousers still soaked in the blood of a dead comrade. These temporary measures were abolished in April 1916, and the pre-war system of courts martial reintroduced. Thereafter, any man found guilty of desertion was sent to the front line. Where, wondered those already serving there, could *they* be sent as punishment?

The front-line soldier might view the enemy without rancour, as a fellow sufferer of appalling living conditions and callous staff officers. 'One poor beggar always sympathizes with another,' commented Captain Paul Rimbault (95th, later 82nd and 74th Infantry). 'And no one more closely resembles the German soldier in his trench than the *poilu* in ours. Poor sods, both.' With the front lines only 20m apart, and listening posts closer still, artillery fire was as likely to hit friend as foe, and many men declined to make life worse by gratuitously opening hostilities. Christmas 1914 certainly saw a truce in the French as well as the British lines: one account from 99th Infantry in Picardy suggests that hostilities were unofficially suspended from Christmas Eve to Twelfth Night. In a quiet sector of the Chemin des Dames in July 1917, Paul Rimbault spotted French and German sentries just 8m apart, 'each sitting on the parapet, the Boche smoking his pipe, the Frenchman writing a letter'. The high command deplored such sentiments. So, too, did Antoine Redier (338th Infantry, later Fourth Army staff), a native of Lille, whose home was occupied by the Germans throughout the conflict: 'In reality, most of our men aren't ready for war,' he railed. 'They fail to grasp that the German is their hereditary enemy. They dislike him as an adversary, but that is not enough ... We must dispel the ridiculous notion that the Germans are men like us.'

Meanwhile other arms of service were maligned as shirkers. 'Corporals and soldiers weren't shirkers,' wrote Georges Demonchy (4th Zouaves). 'They manned the trenches and suffered in them too; they occupied listening posts and went on patrols. But sergeants were shirkers, as were machine-gunners, artillerymen, officers, regimental transport and [all] staffs – regimental, brigade and divisional. The heavy artillery, engineers, aviators, drivers and all the rear services were also dismissed as shirkers by the division, particularly by those at the front.' Harsh words, born of the solidarity of front-line units. Yet while the infantryman undoubtedly bore the brunt of the fighting, the contribution of the wider army cannot be so readily dismissed. Artillery, engineers, aviation, cavalry, transport and other supporting corps – all had a vital role to play in the eventual Allied victory.

Near Petit-Vimy (Pas-de-Calais), 9 December 1915. The degree of mutual sympathy between front-line troops is exemplified here. The Germans have just exploded a mine under the French trenches at Côte 140, at the northern end of Vimy Ridge, but so churned was the ground that neither side could profit from the blast. By tacit agreement, both sides concentrated instead on shoring up their own trenches: the French in the foreground, the Germans to the rear. 'They're still somebody's children, even if they are our enemy,' concluded one French soldier.

Near Longpont (Aisne), 18 July 1918. Enemy prisoners were greatly prized as a source of valuable intelligence. Gas mask over his shoulder, this young German sits outside an aid post, stoically ignoring the stares of the surrounding Frenchmen, probably members of a north African regiment. His shoulder straps have already been removed to identify his regiment.

Near Hardivillers (Oise), 2 April 1918. The Entente Cordiale in action: under the watchful gaze of a group of locals, the men of 45th Artillery share a loaf with some Royal Engineers. On the Somme in 1916, Sylvain Wannenmacher (109th Infantry) took a positive view of his allies: 'That's where we came across our first British soldiers. We're sharing their billets in the village. We like the way they have their comforts organized, even in wartime. They have a central mess where they can stock up: wine, beer, drink of all kinds, cigarettes, canned food. I'm hurrying over to buy some cigarettes, not that I can afford many.' But as the British retreated before the German offensives in the spring of 1918, other Frenchmen thought very differently: 'They're complete swine!' fumed one soldier. 'It's a disgrace.'

Houdelaincourt (Meuse), 26 July 1917. Newly arrived American soldiers meet the men of 12th Chasseurs, both parties appearing resolutely unimpressed by their allies. Georges Cuvier (162nd Infantry) was serving in Lorraine when the first Americans appeared there: 'The countryside, so quiet when we arrived, has become extremely lively since the Americans flooded in. They are kings of all they survey, fêted everywhere, rich as Croesus, wanting only to fraternize.'

Verneuil-Courtonne (Aisne), 1914. A team of seven gunners prepares to fire a 75mm field gun. Left, two men are about to retrieve the appropriate round (shrapnel or explosive) and set the fuse, while ahead of them a third man holds a telephone, waiting for the orders of the battery commander. Centre, wearing a scarf, is the gun-layer, responsible for aiming the weapon. Holding a shell is the loader, who will place it in the open breech, and next to him is the firer, who will close the breech and fire the gun. The gun commander, a sergeant, stands furthest right. The gun, with a range between 8,000 and 11,000m, could in theory fire up to twenty-eight rounds a minute, although its more usual rate was six.

Near Ferme Chavigny (Aisne), 18 July 1918. Although the 75mm field gun was too shallow in trajectory to destroy barbed-wire entanglements, it remained in service throughout the war. Here, a group of guns executes a rolling barrage on the opening day of the second battle of the Marne, supporting 4th Zouaves in their attack on the Bois Mauloy. 4th Zouaves was part of 38th Division, which had to be withdrawn to rest after just a week in this sector of the line.

Near Moulin de Côtelette (Meuse), March 1915. A priest blesses a shell belonging to this battery sited north of Verdun. The battery was equipped with the antiquated Bange 120L, first introduced in 1878. Although big and slow-firing, the Bange was the mainstay of the French heavy artillery during the early years of the war and remained in service even after the introduction of the 155GPF in late 1917.

Near Soupir (Aisne), May 1917. Shells are lined up to the right of this Schneider 155C howitzer, pictured here in action at full recoil. The pre-war French army had rejected howitzers as an encumbrance, but they were built by Schneiders for export to Russia. The advent of trench warfare finally ignited French interest, and the first howitzer-equipped units reached the Western Front in April 1916. Confounding earlier anxieties, the gun proved both mobile and accurate.

Near Saint-Léger-aux-Bois (Oise), June 1918. The 155GPF, designed by Lieutenant Colonel Louis Filloux in response to the urgent need for heavy artillery, was the most modern piece in the French arsenal. Introduced in late 1917, it was accurate and quick-firing (three to four rounds a minute), but most of the production run went to supply the US Army, only 320 examples reaching the French front lines. Captain Charles Delvert was proved correct in his forebodings: 'Our quick-firing 155 could see off the [enemy] 210, but it won't reach the front in sufficient quantity for at least another six months,' he had prophesied in August 1916.

Near Thillois (Marne), April 1917. A 320mm railway gun, one of six constructed using barrels removed from the coastal fortresses at Brest (Finistère) and Cherbourg (Manche). The gun fired a round every five minutes, with a maximum range of about 20km. Railways guns of several different calibres were grouped together in 1917 in a number of specialized units as 70th to 78th Super-Heavy Artillery Regiments.

Near Courmelois (Marne), February 1916. These guns – possibly part of 3rd Battery, 3rd River Artillery Group – are mounted on barges based on the Canal de l'Aisne à la Marne. Sixteen barges entered service in 1915, all crewed by naval personnel. Four of the barges were armed with two 100mm guns apiece; twelve, with a single 140mm gun. With a top speed of 9 knots, they formed a useful mobile artillery reserve, supporting offensives in Champagne and on the Aisne. The batteries were disbanded in late 1917 and their crews returned to sea duty.

Aisne, July 1918. Here, shells are being loaded into the vehicles of TM211. Moving the mountain of ammunition devoured by the guns was a herculean task, requiring sixty convoys a day, each thirty-six lorries strong. Between 1914 and 1918 the French artillery grew inexorably – heavy guns from 300 to 5,200; 75mm field guns from 3,900 to 5,600 – as did its appetite for shells. By September 1914 some 100,000 75mm shells were consumed daily, even then seven times the pre-war estimate and ten times current output. On 20 August 1917, during limited offensives around Verdun, 3 million shells were used, while on 23 September 1918, during the second battle of the Marne, over 1¼ million 75mm shells were fired.

Near Beaurieux (Aisne), May 1917. Schneider diesel *locotracteur* no. 30947 hauls a load of 155mm munitions along a 60cm narrow-gauge railway. The Schneider was one of several engine types, diesel and steam, introduced to supplement the pre-war Péchot steam locomotive. The 60cm network was originally installed to supply frontier fortresses like Verdun, but new lines were quickly added throughout the Western Front. Standard- and metre-gauge railways were the responsibility of 5th Engineers, but these narrow-gauge networks were operated by detachments from 68th and 69th Foot Artillery.

Heippes (Meuse), March 1916. Situated on the *Voie Sacrée*, south of Verdun, and close to the pre-war *Meusien* narrow-gauge railway line, Heippes served as an intermediate depot for the transport of stores and munitions. Here, a munitions convoy is unloaded. Regimental transport, almost entirely horse-drawn, then carried the shells to positions in the front line.

Near Châlons-sur-Vesle (Marne), 21 February 1916. The support offered to front-line trenches by a distant artillery often proved tardy and inaccurate, so the French soon sought a more responsive alternative. Several 'home-made' contraptions were developed to project grenades into enemy trenches, although none proved consistently reliable. Here, Lieutenant Grotard (43rd Infantry) demonstrates a grenade-throwing catapult of his own design.

Near Margival (Aisne), May 1917. Over the winter of 1914/15 arsenals were raided for weapons and museum pieces like this 1880-pattern 220mm Bange mortar were pressed into service. Like its peers, the Bange was heavy and cumbersome; it also took at least twenty-five minutes to set up. A wheeled carriage was introduced in 1917 to increase its mobility and help absorb the recoil, and the Bange continued in use until the armistice.

Near Bitry (Oise), September 1915. Two men load a Cellerier trench mortar. This 65mm weapon was first introduced in November 1914 as a simply made expedient to provide fire support to the infantry; the early examples used discarded German shell cases fixed to a wooden block. Yet it remained in service until 1917, often in batteries of six or twelve.

Vauquois (Meuse), May 1915. The artillery received 115 examples of this 1885-pattern 37mm naval pompom for potential trench use, but they proved too immobile to be effective. They were turned over to aviation instead and fitted into Voisin aircraft.

Near La-Ville-aux-Bois (Aisne), February 1916. Tucked down in a trench near the latrines, two crew members have adopted rather fixed expressions as they prepare to fire another experimental trench mortar, the Guidetti bomb thrower. Two different versions of the Guidetti were produced – 65mm and 77mm – but neither was adopted.

Near Saint-Thomas-en-Argonne (Marne), February 1916. North of the village, on the Servon road, men use foot pumps to refill the reservoir of an 86mm Hachette trench mortar, one of several different prototypes using compressed air as a propellant. Such weapons were quiet and accurate but demanded very careful maintenance by their crews.

Vauquois (Meuse), July 1915. First introduced in April 1915, the 58mm Type 2 eventually became the most widely used trench mortar in the French army, with some 2,440 examples in service. Small and light, it was highly portable and easily manoeuvred in the trench. Its maximum range was about 1,200m and it fired a 20kg bomb.

Near Mont-Chenot (Marne), 27 May 1918. Both sides employed balloons and aircraft to acquire enemy targets behind the front lines. Here, south of Reims, a balloon prepares to ascend on the opening day of the German Blücher-Yorck offensive. The attack took the Germans deep into French lines, but the French resisted on the flanks, surrounding the enemy on three sides – the genesis of the second battle of the Marne in July. The observer (with headphones) and his comrade are armed with a machine gun as protection against enemy fighters on balloon-busting missions. Parachutes, first introduced in 1916, are contained in the separate drum secured to the front of the basket.

Belleville-sur-Meuse (Meuse), January 1916. Adjudant Leroy (pilot), Sergeant Henri Marchand (observer), and Soldier René Forest (mechanic) are pictured (right to left) with their Caudron G3 at this airfield south of Verdun. The trio were members of C18, an army cooperation squadron flying a mixture of Caudron G3 and G4 aircraft on reconnaissance missions for XXX Corps. The squadron was re-equipped with the Salmson 2A2 in February 1918.

Hétomesnil (Oise), 8 May 1918. Staff and pilots of GC12, the celebrated 'Storks', gather on the day René Fonck (standing, sixth from left) downed a record six enemy aircraft in twenty-four hours. Other famous 'Storks' include Joseph Batlle (standing, far left), Jean Bozon-Verduraz (standing, fourth from left), Xavier de Sevin (standing, eighth from left), the Serb Vladislav Sondermayer (behind de Sevin), and the American Frank Baylies (seated, third from right).

Hétomesnil (Oise). Xavier de Sevin was eventually credited with twelve confirmed and thirteen unconfirmed victories. He was the nephew of Major Charles de Rose, the founder of the French fighter arm, and wears the uniform of his original unit, 19th Chasseurs. These twin allegiances are embodied in the pilot's personal insignia painted on his SPAD fighter – a rose within the hunting horn of the chasseurs. The adjacent stork is the emblem of SPA26; each of GC12's four squadrons had its own variant of the bird.

Roissy-en-France, August 1918. Lieutenant James Buis and Sergeant Fernand Gizandin are pictured here with their Breguet XIV bomber. Buis (left), the pilot, was the veteran of fifty-seven missions; Gizandin, the observer, of sixty-five. The crew belonged to squadron BR126, one of the three squadrons in bomber group GB3, then flying daylight missions in support of ground forces during the allied counter-offensives. Roissy airfield is now the site of Charles de Gaulle international airport.

Lunéville (Meurthe-et-Moselle), September 1915. A column of hussars pass bombed-out workshops in the Place des Carmes. Lunéville was the first town in France to be shelled, six bombs falling an hour before the Germans declared war on 3 August 1914. The hussars and the chasseurs à cheval together made up the light cavalry. 'In Givry [Marne], [we] watched 14th Hussars trot past,' noted Charles Delvert in December 1915. 'I recalled the squadrons who marched beside us at the start: monocled officers in sky-blue tunics, shakos with white trim and white plume, martingales linked with copper; the men in red trousers, blue jackets and shakos. . . . Now [both] officers and men were wearing infantry greatcoats, helmets and trousers – a silver number on a black badge the only reminder of the glorious hussars. No, there was something else: their horses. Fine beasts, well groomed despite the long campaign. These were definitely cavalrymen.'

Near Tartigny (Oise), 3 April 1918. Men of 9th Dragoons (5th Cavalry Division) walk their horses along the Breteuil road after seeing action around Roye (Somme) during the German Operation Michael. The regiment was leaving the line to spend a month refitting, before moving south-east to Champagne. Although they had fought dismounted, each man is still carrying his lance. Bamboo lances were issued to some dragoon regiments from 1890, with a new, all-metal pattern – intended for all dragoon, chasseur and hussar regiments within the cavalry divisions – following in 1913. However, few of the latter had been distributed before production ceased in 1915. 'A rotten weapon, heavy and cumbersome,' judged one dragoon officer, 'but terrifying in the hands of anyone who knew how to use it.'

Near Bellacourt (Pas-de-Calais), 1915. The two cuirassiers pictured here are serving in the trenches alongside an infantryman. They have removed the crest from their cavalry helmet and abandoned their steel cuirass. 'We are rather ashamed to be cavalrymen,' admitted Robert Desaubliaux (11th Cuirassiers, later 129th Infantry). 'Our role has been so minor compared to the infantry. ... The cavalry will certainly play no further part in this conflict.' But Desaubliaux soon regretted his decision to request a transfer. 'I made up my mind [ten months ago] to join the infantry. How stupid! I'm kicking myself now.'

Near Bucy-le-Long (Aisne), April 1917. Railway engineers lay a corduroy raft to provide a track-bed for the railway artillery. The standard-gauge lines in Champagne and around Verdun were controlled by 7th Section, 5th Engineers; the metre-gauge lines, like the *Le Meusien*, by 10th Section. The 5th Engineers also supervised the building of new lines, but the work was performed by others: territorial and west African battalions; labourers from Indochina and other colonial possessions, as well as China and Italy; and German prisoners of war.

Révillon (Aisne), September 1916. Beams are cut for trench use in this military sawmill. Vast quantities of wood were consumed during the conflict – to build and reinforce trenches, provide pit-props for mines, construct billets, and supply the aircraft industry. In 1914 government forestry employees were called up regardless, but in 1915/16 they were transferred to the Army Forestry Service, which could better employ their expertise. Divisional, corps and army headquarters all had their own forestry detachments, while the Canadian and American forces also included a large number of forestry troops to guarantee their own supplies.

Souilly (Meuse), March 1916. This type TP lorry no. 51846 (D4) has been converted from a Schneider bus chassis previously operated in Paris by the Compagnie Générale des Omnibus. It forms part of a convoy carrying infantrymen (possibly 255th Infantry) out of the front line at Verdun. The *Voie Sacrée* ran down the main street of Souilly, whose *mairie* was home to Second Army HQ. Bus chassis were converted into a range of vehicles carrying men, munitions, fresh meat and even artillery horses.

Second Army park, Bar-le-Duc (Meuse), May 1918. Clad in voluminous overalls, female mechanics reinstall an engine. The vehicle under shelter is a Peugeot 4-tonne 1525-type lorry, manufactured in great quantity during the conflict. In the background is an Italian Fiat. Army parks undertook light repairs, but anything more serious was referred to a specialist repair park. Nurses apart, it is unusual to see women serving so close to the front line. Qualified mechanics were in short supply throughout the war, and by November 1918 a backlog of some 16,000 vehicles was awaiting repair.

Épernay (Marne), September 1918. A Holt 75 caterpillar tractor hauls a 155L of Battery A (55th Artillery), heading to rest from the front line near Fismes (Marne). The American Holt was a rare sight. Preference was given to vehicles and equipment manufactured by French firms like Schneider and Peugeot, and by November 1918 just nineteen Holt 75s were in service.

Near Port à Binson (Marne), 1915. Despite making extensive use of lorries, the pre-war army still contained over 3 million horses – for cavalry, artillery and transport purpose. Another 750,000 were requisitioned on the outbreak of war, with large numbers later imported to spare French agriculture. Even in 1918 over two million horses remained in service – and every animal had to be fed. Here, a forage convoy hauled by imported Australian oxen makes its way along the road. The harvests were good in 1913 and 1914, but imported oats were required from 1915 onwards, or alternatives like beet were substituted.

Wormhoudt (Nord), 20 May 1918. Horses are requisitioned in the main square before an interested crowd that includes two British officers. Farmers relinquished their horses with a heavy heart. 'Poor beasts, they're helping defend France too,' thought farmhand Louis Duchesne (102nd Infantry). 'Bouleau is going, passed fit for service. His masters were in tears when they gave him a last sugar lump.' A contemporary comic postcard takes up the same theme: 'Keep my husband at the front as long as you like,' the farmer's wife tells the requisitioning officer. 'But leave me the mare!'

Viel-Arcy (Aisne), September 1917. Soldiers weave branches through a wire frame to camouflage a road east of the village. Both sides observed traffic from the air – to gather intelligence or find convoys to shell – and great effort went into screening the most vulnerable sections of road with branches or specially manufactured cloth. From 1916 each army group had its own unit of specialist camouflagers, made up of artists and theatre employees. The cloth was made in Paris by a workforce including Indochinese labourers, German prisoners and over 10,000 women.

Near Valmy (Marne), July 1915. Territorials work hard on road maintenance, using locally quarried ballast wherever possible. The army perfected its traffic management systems during the Champagne offensive of autumn 1915, establishing the basis for the massive resupply effort essential to the defence of Verdun the following year. 'A thaw in one instance, rain in another, poor sub-soil, utter lack of local materials, each theatre of operations offered its own particular challenge,' recalled Lieutenant Colonel Lorieux. 'At Verdun we were faced with the lot: snow, thaw and rain from the last week of February to the end of April. The situation stood on a knife edge.'

Wesserling (Haut-Rhin), February 1918. Drivers plastered with snow fight their way through the icy Vosges mountains in a supply sled. Captain Louis Moufflet (62nd Chasseurs) had been despatched to Alaska in August 1915 to acquire huskies for exactly these conditions. He returned with 400 dogs, soon formed into two dedicated Alaskan Dog Detachments. Ski sleighs were also used to evacuate the wounded from the mountains.

Bar-le-Duc (Meuse), October 1916. Soldiers and postal employees (in smocks) sort mail at the main post office for onward delivery to the front. 'You wouldn't believe how glad we are to receive a parcel,' wrote one front-line soldier. 'We're like big children here. The smallest thing makes us happy or sad. All these family men watch eagerly for the post, waiting for a letter or parcel. What a let-down if they come away empty handed! A letter brings a smile. They rip open the envelope and read it avidly, wiping away a tear with the back of their hand.'

Villers-Allerand (Marne), June 1917. General Philippe Pétain (1856–1951) inspects a unit. Flanked by a phalanx of corps and regimental commanders, Prime Minister Georges Clemenceau paid a similar visit to Henri-Aimé Gauthé (29th Infantry) and his comrades. 'Before this all-seeing, all-hearing council of elders, smiling a smile that threatened reprisals, the poor victim was thoroughly cowed. He could do nothing but say yes to a series of artfully posed questions: Do you think we will be victorious? Do you think the home front will hold? The rations are certainly adequate, are they not, General? All phrased in such a way that the soldier, already struck dumb by his encounter with the hierarchy, had no chance to protest.'

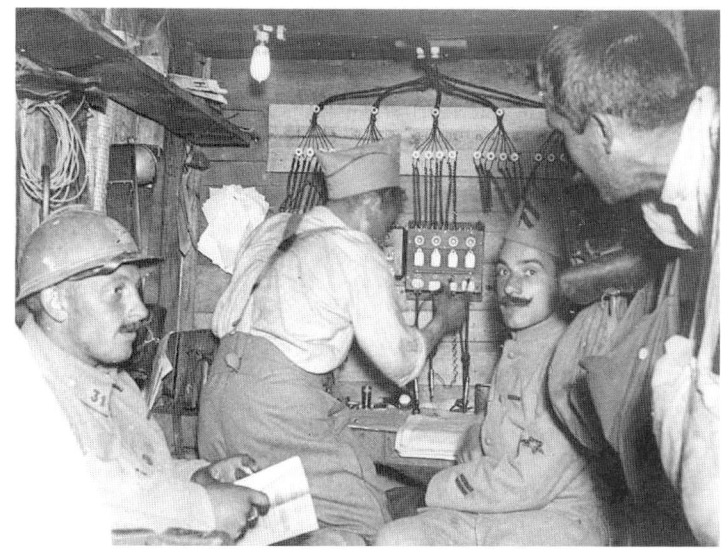

Near Pontavert (Aisne), July 1917. This telephonists' post is situated in a gallery under the Bois des Buttes. Although regimental signallers might appear comfortably ensconced, they also had to venture out into no man's land. 'A telephonist needs plenty of distinctive landmarks he can recognize in the dark,' explained Émile Cartier (127th Infantry), from Verdun. 'His safety often hangs on how quickly he can complete a repair. Shells cut the lines five or six times a day, and as often at night. We bound from shell-hole to shell-hole, armed with a reel of wire and the kit we use to mark breaks. Our bayonet comes in handy as a stake. Although it's winter and still snowing heavily, we often get back to our post in Bras soaked in sweat.'

Fifth Army electrical services park, near Jonchery-sur-Vesle (Marne), September 1917. The kind of living arrangements deeply resented by front-line soldiers, this comfortable dugout, the *Villa Cafardiste*, is amply decorated with prints from *La Vie parisienne*. 'With its Gerda Wegener prints of a girl in corset and bloomers, *La Vie parisienne* is far and away the most popular of the illustrated magazines,' thought Captain Charles Delvert. 'I run across it every time I visit an HQ.... Right now it's raining minnies and heavy shells, but to my right a voluptuous, saucer-eyed blonde draped languorously over an armchair reminds me that elsewhere life goes on; that death and incarceration are reserved for the poilu; that 200km away human beings are enjoying all the pleasures of civilization.'

Chapter Five

'Life goes on'

Fifteen days in the trenches were followed in principle by eight days in reserve. The relief was always an eagerly anticipated, if still perilous, moment. 'We roam around in the dark, splashing through the mud,' reported Louis Mairet (127th Infantry). 'Flares go up, pickets fire; out in no man's land the German patrols are keeping their heads down. The rain is torrential. Finally, the relief gets moving. Packs on! We set off, stumbling through the downpour. Squeeze to one side to allow a section to pass. Off again. Arrive at a crossroads. Wait for 1st Platoon, who don't turn up. Off again to meet the captain on the road. Wait in the rain without removing our packs. He arrives, we set off again, muddy and sodden. Stop at Cauroy. Arrive at Hermonville at two in the morning. Muddy, filthy. Soaked to the bone. Tired. Exhausted. We collapse into some straw. Unless you've experienced a relief, you have no idea!'

Short rest periods (*petit repos*) were spent in the reserve front line, while longer spells (*grand repos*) were passed further to the rear, requiring a trip by lorry or train. The accommodation on offer varied between sectors. In villages and towns sufficiently in the rear to retain some inhabitants, cellars might provide a safe haven. Elsewhere the only bed available might be a pile of rotten, flea-infested straw in the corner of a barn. In sectors with no potential billets, the Engineers were supposed to build barrack huts, but this seldom happened – and certainly not before 1917. Nor did rest periods provide much in the way of relaxation. 'Once we were out of the trenches, our weapons, clothing, boots, hair, feet, field dressings, reserve rations and cartridges were all inspected,' recalled Georges Pineau (44th Chasseurs). 'We stood watch; got vaccinated; peeled potatoes; cleaned the huts; washed our clothes; attended lectures on how to operate a machine gun or wear a gas mask; drums beating, we took part in parades, reviews and ceremonies; and, just to keep our hand in, we went on exercises.'

Home leave was a precious commodity, the more so given its rarity. In 1915 men who had served over a year at the front were granted one six-day leave period every four months – a commitment honoured more in the breach than in the practice. Leave was cancelled on the eve of any major attack; and such was the nature of French strategy in 1915, with attacks taking place right along the line, that unofficially all leave was cancelled – a major grievance for the mutineers of May 1917. Although leave was quickly reinstated by Pétain, its reintroduction only aggravated another long-standing complaint – that of journey times. Wartime service restrictions, compounded by a railway network that directed most passengers via Paris, already cut into precious leave time (counted from the moment a man left his unit); indeed, Corsicans and southerners could spend up to three weeks just in transit. Now, with leave reinstated, the lines became blocked by the huge number of trains entering the capital, forcing men to spend hours waiting at the track side. Leave camps were erected in the suburbs to provide emergency food and shelter, the objections of local politicians doing little to convince fighting men of the depth of civilian support.

'The gap between front and rear stemmed not only from the inequality of risk,' claimed Sous-lieutenant Paul Vaillant-Couturier, later editor of *l'Humanité*. 'It also expressed the gap between two different classes: on one hand, the sacrificed; on the other, those responsible for prolonging that sacrifice.' Visiting the cinema in 1917, Jean Galtier-Boissière (31st Infantry) watched with incredulity as 'bunches of enthusiastic actors moved under a bombardment as if it wasn't there, showing the innocent how to die with a smile on your lips and a hand on your heart while the orchestra plays a waltz'. Meanwhile civilians asked questions of hopeless naivety: 'Do you fight when it's raining? Do you fight on Sundays?'

Yet there was one group of non-combatants with direct experience of the soldier's suffering – those treating and caring for casualties in hospitals in the rear. Furthest forward were the Lines of Communication hospitals (HOE); each had its own small surgical unit and cared for the wounded in tents or huts prior to their onward evacuation by train to one of a network of hospitals throughout France. Temporary military hospitals were opened to supplement the pre-war institutions run by the Army Medical Service, civilian hospitals co-opted, and new 'auxiliary' hospitals created in large public buildings such as schools, hotels, halls and casinos. The three member societies of the French Red Cross – the Société de Secours aux Blessés Militaires (the oldest and largest), the Association des Dames de France (Catholic and aristocratic) and the Union des Femmes Françaises (Protestant and bourgeois) – played a key role in supplying nurses, and also ran many of the auxiliary hospitals. The religious orders also opened a large number of institutions.

South of Aubérive (Marne), September 1915. The supply services were sometimes slow to erect shelters for men resting after duty in the trenches. Here, huddled under their greatcoats, men bivouac in the open in a wood near the Auberge de l'Espérance. The troops retreating to the Marne in August 1914 were equally exposed. 'Many of the men were affected by the heat and fell victim to sunstroke,' reported Sous-lieutenant François Le Lann (65th Infantry). Then the weather turned. 'We bivouacked without tents, in the rain, shivering with cold.'

Somme-Bionne (Marne), October 1915. Every man at this rest camp at least has a tent for shelter. Conditions, however, could be grim. Maurice Bedel (170th Infantry) endured a similar camp in the Argonne. 'This bivouac is indescribable,' he complained. 'Imagine a huge muddy field, two or three square kilometres, a handful of straw huts, a few shelters made of pine bundles – a wretched conglomeration, unspeakably filthy and depressing. The mud is packed with bones, mouldy bread, empty bottles, barrel hoops, tin cans, red trousers, boots, rifles, cooking pots and dressings.'

Near Roucy (Aisne), 23 April 1917. Men wash their clothes in a stream. 'Good news,' crowed Abel Ferry (166th Infantry), 'I have clean sheets. I can't remember taking my clothes off for nearly two months or my boots for a month. I climbed into bed, shouting for joy.'

Saint-Médard (Aisne), August 1915. A good scrub was always relished, even if the spray does threaten to hit this bather right in the face! Fresh water was at a premium in the trenches, with scarcely enough to drink, let alone wash. Captain Georges Gallois (221st Infantry) emerged from the trenches at Verdun in 1916 'mentally drained, with a bushy beard, a filthy, muddy greatcoat ... stiff legs and a dislocated knee. But a good scrub and two days lying on a palliasse have helped to restore my morale ... And today, like everyone else, I'm fine ... completely relaxed since we're out of hearing of the guns.'

Near Arcis-le-Ponsart (Marne), July 1917. The cooks of 231st Infantry peel potatoes at this rest camp, with their mobile cookers to the rear. 'We all have to contribute to our humble dinner preparations, and each man normally presents his share in his kepi. But some of the veterans are quite happy to appoint the new recruits to replace them in this communal endeavour, smoke a pre-prandial cigarette and wait for the bugler to sound Cookhouse.'

Jonchery-sur-Vesle (Marne), August 1917. The 7,000l of wine carried by this tanker wagon is transferred to smaller barrels for distribution to individual regiments. The army had 4,000 such wagons, supplying twenty-three depots. Six million hectolitres (nearly 132 million gallons) of wine were ordered from Languedoc wholesalers in 1916, and double that amount in 1917, requiring imports from other Mediterranean countries, as well as south America, to meet the demand.

Plessis-de-Roye (Oise), October 1916. Men of the Foreign Legion enjoy a hand of cards in the ruins of the château. Although the scene of heavy fighting in 1914 and 1918, the village was then in a quiet sector. The card games favoured by soldiers included *banque* (gambling on a single card drawn from a full pack) and *manille* (a trick-taking game using a 32-card pack).

Montgobert (Aisne), January 1916. These men of the Foreign Legion are fishing with rod and line, but others preferred more unconventional methods. In 1916 Jean Marot (334th Infantry) was serving on the Somme. 'To supplement our rations, the company's bright sparks are fishing in the Largue, which has exquisite salmon-trout and carp,' he reported. 'They toss a couple of grenades in the river, then jump in and collect anything that floats, diving where necessary to retrieve any big fish merely stunned by the explosion. They've carried an old stove back to the village and use it to deep-fry their 15kg of fish in beef dripping deliberately reserved for the purpose. They make quite a sight, these big lads, laughing and joking round the frying pan, stark naked under their greatcoats, hairy legs exposed to the sun.'

Pont-Arcy (Aisne), August 1915. Adjudant Tourcelles (267th Infantry), founder of the trench newspaper *Marmita*, is seen hard at work outside his homely dugout. The first issue, 'a burst of laughter amid the shell-bursts', was published on 10 January 1915; the last, number 30, appeared on 1 June 1918. As many as 450 different trench newspapers were launched during the war: some lasted only a few issues; others like *Le Crapouillot* continued well into the 1920s.

Near Châlons-le-Vergeur (Marne), June 1917. One man and his dog relax at this rest camp in the woods. Domestic animals were barred by regulations from the front lines; indeed, pets acquired by the Foreign Legion's Garibaldi Battalion were put down for this reason in 1915. Nevertheless, abandoned dogs and cats were often adopted by front-line soldiers, good 'ratters' being particularly prized. Unofficially, greater latitude was granted to pets kept by officers, and to the mascots of artillery batteries.

Sapicourt (Marne), October 1917. A tense moment as distances are calculated in a game of pétanque between two units from eastern France – 230th Infantry from Annecy (Haute-Savoie) and 50th Chasseurs from Saint-Dié (Vosges).

South of Craonelle (Aisne), April 1916. Abbé Bergey, unofficial chaplain of 30th Infantry Division, conducts an open-air mass outside the Château Le Blanc Sablon. French regulations banned regimental padres, except in divisional stretcher-bearer units. 'The padre celebrated a big open-air mass every Sunday, helped by the other priests in my divisional bearer group,' recalled Frédéric Moissonnet (153rd Division). 'There were a lot [of priests] in my group, like all the medical formations, especially the field ambulances. So the divisional bearer group was not the nest of bandits alleged by my CO ... Unless, of course, this senior officer – a dyed-in-the-wool anti-clerical – considered all churchmen bandits. These simple ceremonies were very well attended; nor were they lacking in beauty, including a veteran staff captain who belted out military hymns.'

Wesserling (Haut-Rhin), December 1917. Sheltered in the Thur valley, this small town became the forward depot for the Vosges front. Here, a scene from the revue *Il y a le barbelé* plays before a full house in the garrison theatre. 'What could we do to amuse ourselves and pass the time in the evening?' reminisced General Doreau. 'Getting together to sing or listen to a vocalist was one obvious answer. That's why the earliest events of an artistic nature . . . consisted of spontaneous gatherings of unoccupied soldiers around a performer. Some were talented singers, since professionals were mobilized along with everyone else, but others were no more than enthusiastic.' Fernand Maret (130th Infantry), however, was unimpressed by such theatricals: 'They've organized a little do for the regiment today; they're trying anything to improve morale. Not that I'm interested. Exercises will be cancelled, that's all I'm bothered about.'

Fismes (Marne), August 1915. Men assemble in the main street en route to the station to set off on leave. Situated between Reims and Soissons, Fismes quickly became an important junction for newly laid standard- and metre-gauge lines. Leave was keenly anticipated, but some men faced a sad homecoming. 'The place is just a heap of rubble . . . the square, a complete wreck,' mourned Gabriel Berthout, a grocer's son from Moreuil (Somme). 'Nothing remains of our poor old house, just a jumble of bricks. The only things still standing are five or six cast-iron pillars from the shop at the rear.'

Creil (Oise), May 1918. Scottish volunteers had operated this station canteen since taking over from the French in October 1917, but they would soon be evacuated in the face of the advancing Germans. They were open from 3.00pm to 8.00am and served between 1,500 and 2,000 cups of tea a day. The American Mary Dexter served at HOE6 in Creil as a volunteer ambulance driver with SSY3. 'I have just been into the station yard – to the Scottish Women's Canteen – to get a cup of tea,' she told her mother in February 1918. 'It's very nice to be a poilu and able to use the canteen! It is free, and we are not allowed to pay – the tea isn't bad.'

Gare de l'Est, Paris, January 1916. Laden with haversacks, stick in hand, or wrapped in a hand-knitted scarf, men on leave gather outside the station, their muddy boots suggesting they have just arrived from the front line. Sylvain Wannenmacher (109th Infantry) found it hard to readjust to metropolitan life: 'Life goes on as if nothing unusual is happening. . . . I can't bear it. It's too brutal, indecent to eyes still full of what we've just been through. . . . Boots encrusted with Somme mud, haversack on one shoulder, canteen on the other, clothes ridden with lice, I set off towards the Gare de Lyon. I cut a sorry figure crossing Paris alongside all the shiny, polished shirkers.'

Vendresse-et-Troyon (Aisne), August 1915. A pair of soldiers pause for a snap at the barracks gate. The photographer (second left) lies ready with his camera on a stand. 'Soldiers are among the most fervent devotees of the picture postcard, keen to give their family and friends an idea of the town and its main sights. They particularly favour photographs of the barracks, carefully selecting a shot that shows their own block. They also like scenes that give a glimpse of regimental life. But above all they want their portrait in uniform. The more affluent are the first to succumb, but few men fail to leave a copy of their image with the garrison photographer ...'

Pommiers (Aisne), July 1917. Soldiers help bring in the harvest. With all able-bodied men in the army, France was acutely short of farm labour. Women, children and the elderly filled the breach, then prisoners of war were used, but still more hands were needed. From 1915 older men, territorials in particular, were granted home leave to help with the harvest, and by 1917 whole companies could be detached from their regiment for agricultural work in the rear. Many soldiers came from farming stock, including a Beauceron who served under Charles Delvert (101st Infantry). 'Turned out nice again, sir!' he greeted his captain one fine May morning in 1916. 'A good day to be in the fields with your dog at your side, checking to see if the wheat is coming through.'

Meuse, February 1918. These gunners from 233rd Artillery are returning from leave to Verdun aboard the *Meusien* metre-gauge railway, a pre-war line built to link the small communities between Bar-le-Duc and Verdun. During the battles of 1916 and 1917 it performed a vital role carrying food, munitions and men to the front, and returning with casualties.

Blérancourt (Aisne), October 1917. At this army cider works, soldiers press apples gathered from abandoned farms. Many Breton and Norman soldiers preferred cider to wine and, at the colonel's discretion, it could be issued as part of the rations.

Verberie (Oise), November 1916. Some men found themselves in the rear for reasons other than leave or injury. Pictured here are the judges at a court martial. The presiding officer (third left) was usually a lieutenant colonel, the rest of the panel consisting of a major, a captain, a lieutenant and an NCO. An officer with legal experience was appointed prosecutor. He was assisted by two clerks – one came from the judge-advocate's department, while the other was a volunteer, also with legal experience. Defending counsel was chosen by the accused from a divisional list.

Bar-le-Duc (Meuse), April 1916. Casualties (including a man from 60th Infantry) gather outside HOE20 to await evacuation to the rear. Each has a card pinned to his greatcoat giving details of his diagnosis and onward destination. HOE20 was overwhelmed by casualties during the opening weeks of the battle of Verdun and other hospitals were opened to assist – HOE15 at nearby Revigny-sur-Ornain, and HOE6 at La Queue-de-Mala, closer to the city. Furthest left, identifiable by his collar tabs, is a doctor. Two clerks (second left, and right in doorway) are also present: they belong to 21st Administration Section (COA).

Bar-le-Duc, 12 March 1916. A British Red Cross motor ambulance brings casualties to the station. Each vehicle could carry four men on stretchers or eight seated. Six British volunteer ambulance units – SSA1, SSA2, SSA10, SSA16, SSA17 and SSA18 – served in the Verdun sector during 1916.

Château de la Mothe, Houdancourt (Oise), 1918. These four motor ambulance drivers of the Hackett Lowther Unit (SSY3) have just received the Croix de guerre. The unit was attached to II Corps (Third Army) and was composed largely of British volunteers. The CO, Lieutenant May 'Toupie' Lowther (left), was a champion pre-war tennis player and fencer; Frances Donisthorpe (right) was one of her assistant directors. The GMC lorry, presented by Miss E. Dexter, was one of the unit's twenty or so ambulances. All were painted grey, with the Red Cross and the donor's name on the side, and ranged from heavy vehicles, like this GMC, to big cars – including Toupie's own 6-cylinder Wolseley.

Vadelaincourt (Meuse), October 1916. Men wait outside the huts of HOE12 for evacuation by train. Situated some 15km south-west of Verdun, close to road and rail, and safe from enemy shelling, the hospital opened in late 1915. Between February and June 1916 10,800 men underwent surgery there, 935 dying of their wounds. The vast majority of casualties had suffered shell wounds, a quarter sustained to the head and chest. One medical officer described another HOE at Bouleuse (Marne): '[It was] an immense number of wooden huts camped in the middle of a field, lacking all style or elegance: duckboards for paths . . . Sky full of electricity cables and telephone wires. An impression of order, feverish activity and impermanence all at the same time.'

Soissons (Aisne), August 1916. The network of military hospitals depended on volunteer nurses serving under the aegis of the French Red Cross. Here, Madame Macherez and Mademoiselle Sellier, working under shellfire just behind the front lines in Soissons, and each decorated with the Croix de guerre, are seen in their P2 gas masks. 'The night before last we were gas shelled all night, had to wear our gas masks for five hours,' wrote English volunteer Katherine Hodges. 'Perfectly awful, you feel you can't breathe in the beastly things.'

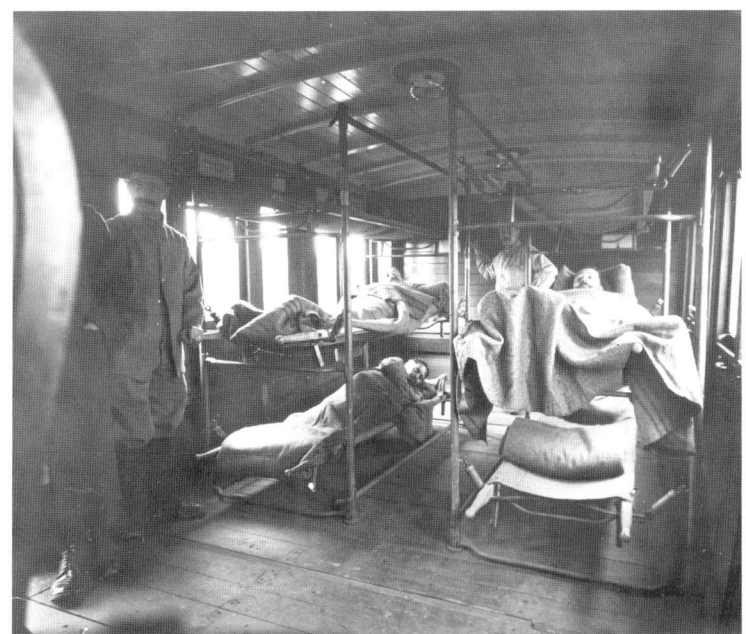

Le Bourget (Seine-Saint-Denis), January 1916. Stretcher cases arrive in the Paris suburbs aboard a medical train. Around 163 trains served the front lines, composed largely of rolling stock requisitioned from the major French railway companies: Paris-Lyon-Méditerranée, Midi, Nord, Est, État and Paris-Orléans. Each train carried around 250 casualties. Around a third were stretcher cases, travelling in converted goods wagons or, as here, in third-class carriages; the rest rode in ordinary passenger carriages. Each train also included a kitchen wagon and a still-room which doubled as a bandaging wagon. Men wounded in Champagne could be in a Paris hospital within forty-eight hours.

Temporary Hospital 104, Angicourt (Oise), November 1917. This convalescent hospital was opened in a local sanatorium. The French did not issue a hospital uniform, but nearly every man here has received a standard white cloth nightcap. Soldier Surle (58th Territorials) was wounded at Verdun: 'Then after hospital came convalescence! What a joy to be in nice clean clothes again! But my [biggest] surprise came when they took me into the mess hall, and I found a plate, cutlery and a napkin at my place; I burst into tears, scarcely able to believe my eyes.'

75 Rue de Reuilly, Paris, April 1916. A cooperage workshop was among the facilities provided at this rehabilitation centre for the war blinded. In January 1916 disabled war veterans were treated by a network of 45 physiotherapy and 10 're-education' centres. By 1917 the latter had grown in number to 160, either government funded or privately sponsored. Approximately half were directed towards the agricultural trades.

Hôpital de Saint-Nicolas, Issy-les-Moulineaux (Hauts-de-Seine), October 1916. Burns are treated using 'ambrine', a proprietary mixture of vaseline, paraffin and antiseptics, originally devised by retired naval surgeon Dr Barthe de Sandfort to treat rheumatism. 'Ambrine' remained a proprietary brand throughout the conflict, but all the Allies devised similar salves, like No. 7 Paraffin.

Military Hospital 5A, Saint-Maurice (Val de Marne), March 1916. Originally opened as a civilian convalescent home in 1858, this hospital had specialized in prosthetics since 1900 and ran its own dedicated workshop, pictured here. Of the three million French soldiers wounded during the war, approximately 300,000 suffered some form of permanent disability.

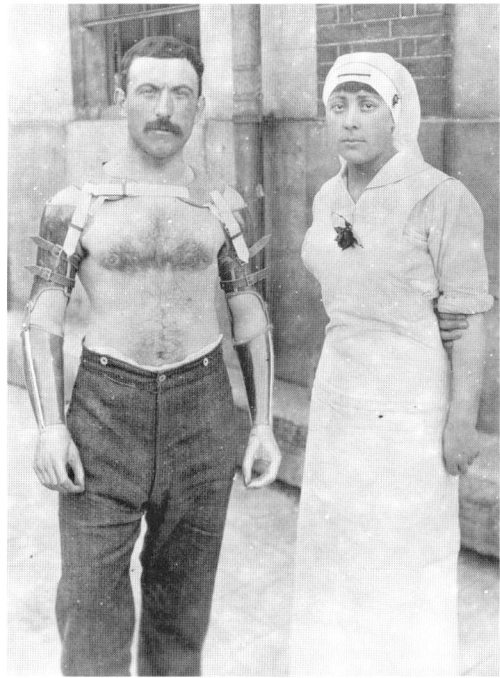

Military Hospital 5A, Saint-Maurice (Val de Marne), June 1916. Soldier Bravais lost both forearms in the conflict and has been fitted with artificial limbs attached to a Deleuny harness. The following month, MO Lucien Laby (294th Infantry) was serving in an aid post at Verdun: 'A young corporal came up to me, alone, both hands severed at the wrist. He stared at the two awful red stumps. Seeking some words of consolation, I asked him what he did in civilian life. His answer made further words redundant. "Sculptor," he replied.'

Auxiliary Hospital 9, Champrosay (Essonne), October 1917. This convalescent hospital was first opened in 1893 by a Catholic nursing order, the Oeuvre de Villepinte, as a girls' sanatorium. The building was requisitioned on the outbreak of war, and many of the nuns remained to care for the new patients. Men are pictured here in the ceramics workshop; other recuperating soldiers were found employment in the hospital gardens.

Chapter Six

'An unforgettable day'

By November 1918 the victorious French army was one of the largest in the world, with almost 5 million men in uniform, compared to 3.6 million in 1914. But army and nation alike were exhausted. The Spanish flu pandemic of 1918/19 compounded the death toll imposed by the war, while almost half the survivors had been wounded – 20 per cent of them twice, and some 100,000 three times or more. In his post-war memoirs Admiral Pierre Ronarc'h, commander of a naval brigade in the desperate battles along the river Yser in 1914/15, and later of French naval forces in the eastern Channel, spoke for many of his countrymen: 'I hope, indeed I am certain, that France will not in the near future experience another conflagration like the Great War. If it should happen again, the human race really must be insane.'

Demobilization began almost immediately. The oldest men were released in December 1918; the class of 1913, the last of the pre-war classes, in August 1919. The wartime classes of 1914 to 1917 rejoined civvy street later that year, but the classes of 1918 and 1919 had to serve out their full three-year engagement. Each man received a demobilization grant of 250 francs plus an additional 20 francs for every month spent in uniform. He could also choose between a suit of clothes or 52 francs in lieu, and if he so wished, was allowed to keep his helmet.

For many men disenchanted with military life, 'idling' away their time in garrisons in occupied Germany (or worse still, fighting the Bolsheviks in Russia, Poland and Ukraine), the process was too slow. Emboldened into candour by the end of hostilities, one man from 230th Infantry addressed his captain: 'We may have won the war, sir, but it's no thanks to you.' He was immediately court-martialled and sentenced to death: 'That really put me in the cart,' he later commented drily. French sailors in Bizerta (Tunisia) demonstrated for their release, as did soldiers closer to home in Toulouse and freezing in far-off Murmansk, where 21st Colonial Infantry mutinied in January 1919. One of their spokesmen summed up their grievances: 'The newspapers now reaching us report the words addressed to parliament by the minister of war, "Since 11 November the sound of gunfire has ceased for all Frenchmen." Here, weeks later, the enemy has just fired a thousand rounds in twenty-four hours! Surely, we too are Frenchmen?'

Veterans like Jacques Meyer (329th Infantry) knew no civilian could ever understand what the soldier had suffered. 'War, you know what that means,' he wrote to an old comrade. 'But once we are dead and gone, what then? War, old chap. It's our buried past, our secret youth.' Some inevitably found it hard to readjust to everyday life. 'I got home in August 1919, and it took me at least a year to settle down,' admitted one man of the class of 1912 (81st Infantry). 'Everything was a mystery to me.' Employers were legally obliged to rehire their former workers, but only if the soldier applied by registered post within a fortnight of returning home. Many forgot, while others found their old firm had closed or that it refused to sack those who had stepped into the breach. 'We have an obligation towards them,' prime minister Georges Clemenceau notably declared of veterans, but many old soldiers believed they had to fight for every entitlement, while half a million returning prisoners of war were more bitter still; they felt mistrusted, almost as if they had surrendered to the enemy.

Among those prisoners was a young Captain Charles de Gaulle (33rd Infantry). Writing from his camp in October 1918, the future French president summed up the profound effects of the war on his nation: 'How will France quickly, if ever, forget a million and a half war dead; a million disabled; Lille, Dunkirk, Cambrai, Douai, Arras, Saint-Quentin, Laon, Soissons, Reims, Verdun in ruins? Will weeping mothers suddenly dry their tears, orphans cease to be orphans, widows cease to be widows? Will not every family in the land, generation after generation, bequeath powerful memories of this greatest of wars, sowing in the hearts of their children seeds of a hatred impossible to eradicate? . . . Each of us knows, each of us senses that this peace is but a thin veil shrouding unsatisfied ambitions, hatreds more stubborn than ever, national wrath that smoulders still.'

Oise, 14 October 1918. Newly liberated civilians greet the advancing French troops in a village north of Soissons. In March 1917 the inhabitants of nearby Noyon had been equally quick to fly the flag: 'People wept, they were frightened. The [Germans] left on Saturday, 17 March . . . [Their] hurried departure in the dead of night seemed a good omen. . . . We cheered [our cavalry] as soon as we dared. And we knew where to find the French flags we'd hidden away and hung them at our windows.'

Paris, 11 November 1918. Crowds celebrate the armistice in the Place de l'Opéra. 'On the boulevards, between two and four o'clock, you never saw so many soldiers – British, American, Belgian, Italian, even French – rushing to kiss the girls! And how sweetly the girls accorded the innocent favour requested by the victors. Indeed, they didn't always wait to be asked.' Among those crowds was Élise Bidet, whose brother was still at the front: 'This is the victory that seemed impossible last June, even as late as 15 July,' she wrote. 'Who could've dared to hope we would now be enjoying such a complete triumph. The gun and bells announced the news in Paris at 11 o'clock. Immediately, everyone was given the day off; immediately, the streets were packed.'

Strasbourg (Bas-Rhin), 21 November 1918. French tricolours adorn the Place Kléber. A short-lived revolutionary council seized power in the city in the days following the armistice and proclaimed the Republic of Alsace Lorraine – only for it to be dissolved as soon as the French troops moved in. 'The weeks preceding the [final] liberation of 22 November 1918 were chaotic, marked by mass movements, processions, demonstrations, looting, fighting and gunfire, but also by scheming, debate, subterfuge and double dealing,' recalled Robert Heitz. '[It is] a web whose threads are hard to disentangle, especially as none of the leading players in this local tragicomedy ... left a full account of events.'

Strasbourg (Bas-Rhin), 21 November 1918. Armed with sledge-hammers, men attack the statue of Kaiser Wilhelm in the Place de la République (the former Kaiserplatz). The Kaiser's head was subsequently laid at the feet of the monument to General Jean-Baptiste Kléber, the French hero of the Revolutionary Wars.

Strasbourg (Bas-Rhin), 22 November 1918. General Gouraud takes the salute of French troops parading before the old Imperial Palace in the Place de la République. The men of 47th Infantry had arrived in town the previous day: 'We marched across the city from the Porte de Schirmeck to the Imperial Palace, passing of course through the Place Kléber. We marched eight abreast, unable to maintain any sort of order in our columns as young Alsatians were continually joining us and taking us by the arm. Within minutes my platoon was twice its normal size, including as many girls as poilus. The pavements were packed, everyone laughing and crying, showering us with flowers and cigars.'

Pfaffenhoffen (Bas-Rhin), December 1918. French prisoners of war linger in their hut in this German camp in Alsace. Captured in the Argonne in 1915, Louis Rives (126th Infantry) was held in several different camps: 'Each man was master of a section of ceiling as large as his palliasse. He guarded this space jealously, lovingly filling it according to the whims of his ingenuity and imagination. It was his own little world, immune to the touch of the passer-by, visible only to him, a privilege impossible to confiscate.'

Near Forbach (Moselle), 4 December 1918. A column of prisoners of war makes its way home to France. These men were fortunate to be released so quickly; others did not return until January 1919. Ambroise Harel (47th Infantry) was shocked by the welcome awaiting him in Dunkirk: 'We always believed France would show every sympathy for the sufferings of its prisoners of war. We could see French soil, so eagerly anticipated. Soon we were going to touch it! Emotions were running high. We had tears in our eyes. We drew alongside! On the quay, bayonets fixed, stood officers and men from regiments in III Corps. No sign of a band. A general frostiness, much to our bewilderment. When I spotted the welcoming party, I moved to the prow. "The Marseillaise! The Marseillaise!" I bellowed. But no! No honours for us. We didn't deserve them! We hadn't been killed, just taken prisoner!'

Paris, February 1919. A newly demobilized soldier tries on his government-issue suit. The garments were manufactured in haste, often simply by dyeing a uniform, and few men took up the offer, afraid the suit would identify them in the streets. For years afterwards it was sardonically known as a 'Clemenceau'.

Paris, February 1919. Newly demobbed soldiers are handed their government grant by men of 20th General Staff and Recruitment Section, based at barracks in the Rue Babylone.

Paris, 14 July 1919. Marshal Joffre and Marshal Foch lead the traditional Bastille Day parade through the Place de l'Opéra. Crowds, including a waiter in his long white apron, pack the balconies and hang from the first-floor windows of the famous Café de la Paix: 'What a wonderful sight on the Place de la Concorde … What an unforgettable day. What will it be like when the troops march through the Arc de Triomphe?' enthused one onlooker. But the *Journal des mutilés*, the principal organ of wounded veterans, struck a more sombre note: 'The celebrations of 14 July 1919 will consecrate [our] victory. May they be splendid, may they be glorious, but may they also sound the death knell for any form of military ceremonial.'

Paris, 14 July 1919. At the very head of the parade was a group of severely disabled veterans. 'If you see a military ceremony, make yourself scarce,' insisted the writer Alain, the pseudonym of Émile Chartier (3rd Artillery). 'If you must stay, think of the dead. Count their number. Remember the war blinded, that will cool the blood. And for those who mourn, instead of getting drunk on glory, have the courage to be sad.'

Paris, 14 July 1919. A legless veteran sells favours to the crowds on the Champs Élysées. A journalist reported a similar encounter in 1917: '"Take one," [he] mumbled, registering my surprise and lack of enthusiasm. "I make them myself." . . . If you try hard enough, you might succeed in turning a blind eye to these living reproaches to our selfishness and ingratitude . . . Military medal, two palms, they deserve more than this pathetic trade in cockades, ill-disguised begging, driven by poverty.'